Elementary 4-5 Book One
The Elements of Art and Composition

Written by Brenda Ellis
Developed by Brenda Ellis and Daniel D. Ellis
Edited by Ariel DeWitt and Daniel D. Ellis
Illustrations and Cover art by Brenda Ellis
Student artists are acknowledged beside their works as they appear in the text.

Third Edition

ACKNOWLEDGMENTS

Thanks to my husband, Daniel Ellis, for his valuable input into this curriculum and for taking care of a multitude of other tasks to make sure this project was completed. Thanks to Christine Ann Feorino for her suggestions and editing in our first edition. Thanks to all the students from Moriah Christian School in grades 4-6 for their enthusiastic participation in these units! Thanks to the other students who worked through the units independently and allowed us to share their work with others through this book. Thanks to Dover Publications Inc., NY and Art Resources, NY for supplying the fine art images by the great masters.

Copyright © 1999, 2008, 2013 by Brenda Ellis

All rights reserved. No portion of this book may be reproduced - mechanically, electronically, or by any other means including photocopying. Don't compromise the educational value of this book by photocopying images. Children cannot see what a pencil drawing should look like when tonal values are reduced to black and white.

Printed in the U.S.A.
ISBN: 978-1-939394-04-0

Published by
Artistic Pursuits Inc.
Northglenn, Colorado
www.artisticpursuits.com
alltheanswers@artisticpursuits.com

Getting Started

CONTENTS

Page	Unit	
2		Contents/ Art Supplies
3		What Parents Want to Know Book Content and Scheduling
4		What Students Want to Know The Mysterious Language of Art
5		**The Elements of Art**
6	1	Space
11	2	Line and Shape
16	3	Texture
21		The Elements Combined- Line, Shape, and Texture
22	4	Value
27	5	Form
32	6	Form using Value
37	7	Local Value
42		The Elements Combined- Values and Forms
43	8	Contrast
48	9	The Shapes of Natural Forms
53	10	Edges
58		**Composition**
59	11	Balance
64	12	Rhythm
69		The Elements Combined- Solid and Textured Areas
70	13	Overlap
75	14	Depth
80	15	Proportion, the Face
85		The Elements Combined- Lines, Forms, and Values
86	16	Movement
91		Evaluation Sheet
92		Bibliography

ART SUPPLIES

Units 1-7:
4 - Ebony pencils
1 - vinyl eraser
1 - metal pencil sharpener
1 - sketch pad for drawing
1 - paper sack
1- drawing board (optional)

Unit 8:
4- sheets of scratch-art paper (black on white or colored background)

Units 9-10: additional supplies
1- white colored pencil (Prismacolor)
8- sheets black construction paper
1-scissors
1-glue stick

Units 11-16: additional supplies
1 - Pigma Graphic marker 1mm
      (pointed tip marker)
1 - Pigma Graphic marker 2mm
      (flat tip marker)
1-ruler

DRAWING BOARD: A drawing board can be purchased at art supply stores, or can be cut from a small piece of 3/8 inch hardboard, found in lumberyards. Cut it to 15"x 16" for a small board, or 18" x 18" for a medium board. It is portable so you can draw anywhere.

2

Getting Started

What Parents Want to Know
Book Content and Scheduling

Artists have always focused on two groups of topics known as the elements of art and principles of design when learning to draw. These are the chosen topics of each unit in this book. Each topic is explored in four unique ways. This gives students enough experience with the topic that they naturally incorporate it into the way that they draw. It becomes part of their thinking as they draw any kind of subject matter. This kind of focus, and many opportunities to practice, is how children learn to draw.

Building a Visual Vocabulary   First Page of Each Unit

Here students are shown which topic to focus on, explained in words and pictures. The creative exploration assignment guides students to observe the topic in their own environment, make connections to real-world experiences, and create a work of art from their observations and ideas.

American Art Appreciation and History   Second and Third Page of Each Unit

Students are shown how the topic is used in master works and apply their new observations to a work of art that they create. Students also learn about artists and the times they lived in.

Techniques   Fourth Page of Each Unit

Students learn how to use the materials and tools of art. They apply that knowledge to make original works.

Application   Fifth Page of Each Unit

Students do a final project incorporating new techniques and application of the topic. They use a variety of references such as still life objects, landscapes, portraiture, photographs and more!

Scheduling Art Class Using this Book for One Full School Year

CLASSES PER WEEK: TWO   **CLASS TIME: ONE HOUR**

This schedule can be modified to fit yours. Keep in mind that students can work independently so it is their time you are scheduling, not your own. Schedule art class at a time when they can complete the art assignment, even if it runs over an hour. Once interrupted, students can rarely return to an activity with as much enthusiasm as they first had. The amount of time for completing each activity will vary greatly, depending on the student's experience and personality. However, you should see that as they learn to use more of the elements within their pictures that they are taking more time on each piece. A goal would be to work up to spending one hour on a project by the end of the year.

Getting Started

What Students Want to Know

THE MYSTERIOUS LANGUAGE OF ART

If the secrets of great artists were contained in a book, would you open it? We hope your answer is YES! There is much to learn from artists who have created all their lives. The first great secret artists share with others is:

1. Learn to observe the world around you- to really see it.

"OK", you say, "I'm looking and I see the same things I've always seen." We won't let you be stuck there. The second part of this secret is:

2. Learn *what* to look for.

We tend to look at subject matter and make vague and arbitrary decisions about what we see. Comments such as "grass is green," "faces are hard to draw," "I can draw a horse from the side, but not from the front," all show that we are focusing on our ideas about the subject, and not on what we see. If you've ever made statements similar to these, you are simply focusing on the wrong type of information. As you look at the world in the ways artists do, your art will greatly improve. This book is designed to show you just what those ways are.

Do artists really *see* differently? After all, we all have the same kind of eyes and unless impaired in some way, we do see the same as everyone else. So artists see the same as everyone else, but they have learned to focus on a particular aspect of what they see, and at the same time block out other types of information. The language of art includes code words called the elements of art. You may have heard about these elements, which include space, line, shape, texture, form, value, and color. The third part of that secret tells us how to see the world using the elements of art.

3. Learn to *focus* on one element of art at a time, while drawing, and *block out* the others.

With practice, your mind can focus on any element of art you choose. Your mind can switch with lightning speed to any other element and back again or onto another. This makes it a powerful focusing and blocking out tool.

4

THE ELEMENTS OF ART

In the units ahead, you will learn that artists can draw an object in different ways by focusing on the elements of art. The dogs below show what can happen when one element of art is focused on at a time. You'll have opportunity to use space, line, shape, texture, value, and form separately and all together. This art program may not be like others you have seen. We do not ask you to copy illustrations within the book. Instead, you will draw things that appeal to you, within the context of each unit. It is part of the creative process to choose your subject and how you want to draw it.

We challenge you to try new subject matter and new ways of working. You will be asked to draw from memory, from your imagination, and much of the time from observing a real object. The results of working in these three ways will be very different. Observation work will look more realistic than what comes from the other two ways of working because you will have all the details in front of you. Memory drawing trains your mind to hold onto visual information. Imagination drawing requires that you make-up a narrative that you can see in your mind, change, and build on. Give each project your best effort and we are sure you will be surprised at how much creative talent you have. For inspiration, we show you lots of artwork from the great masters of American Art and from students just like you. We are all creative beings. You are on a journey to explore that part of yourself.

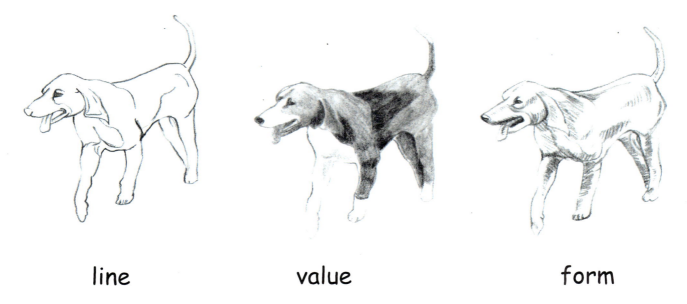

line   value   form

UNIT 1   space   Lesson 1

The white area of the paper is the **space** you draw into.

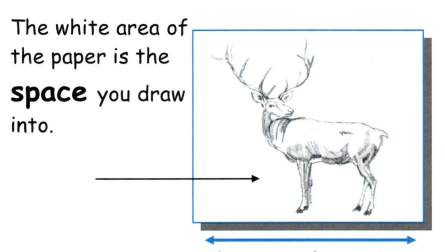

The space can be turned in a **horizontal position** or a **vertical position**. It should be turned to best fit the subject.

Explore Your World! A CREATIVE EXERCISE USING REAL-WORLD EXPERIENCE

A story is often told about two frogs that fell into a large bucket of cream. The first frog saw that there was no way to hop out of the white fluid, accepted his fate, and drowned. The second frog began thrashing about. He tried every way he could think of to stay afloat. He thought that if he could just stay afloat long enough, a solution would come. After a while, his churning turned the cream to butter. That's how we get butter you know, not with frogs, but by stirring up the cream. The frog climbed on the solid mass forming around him and eventually hopped out (Von Oech 192).

A blank sheet of white paper can be just as scary to you as the white cream was to the frogs. The first frog said, "I can't do it." The second frog said, "I'll try something!" Take the second frog's approach. Try new things. Thrash about for a while. Connect the pencil to paper and **move your hand around**! In time, you will see success for your efforts.

TRY IT: Look for a subject that seems simple but interesting. While looking at the object, draw the outside edge of the object. Objects like kitchen chairs, action figures, model machinery, and plants have strange and unusual edges. Drawing, while looking closely at an object's edge, trains your mind and hand to work together. The Ebony pencil will make a very dark mark, or with less pressure, a lighter mark.

OBJECTIVE: to try new ways of drawing and eliminate any fears associated with doing it right or perfectly. The act of drawing is a great way to build better eye/hand coordination skills.

Looking at Space in Art   Lesson 2

Think about your paper as a space your subject will fit in. If the subject is wide or long, like this boat full of troops, then position the paper horizontally. The wide picture space allows the boat to move around by having space in the front and back. We feel when looking at it that the boat moves forward because it has room to do so.

Emmanuel Leutze (1816-1868). *Washington Crossing the Delaware*, 1851. Photo Credit: Dover Publications Inc.

Problems with Space

If the spaces on both sides of the boat are shortened, the boat looks as if it is stuck between the edges of the painting. The men seem to be pushing to get the boat moving. In order to **cross** the river, the boat needs room to move about the picture space.

A figure is taller than it is wide. General George Washington wishes that this artist had considered the vertical position before placing him in this picture space.

General George Washington now has room to stand tall because the picture space is in the vertical position.

THE ARTIST: Emanuel Gottlieb Leutze (LOIT suh) (1816-1868), American/German painter

Leutze spent his childhood in the United States after he and his parents emigrated from Germany. He learned to draw on his own while staying beside the bed of his sick father. Later he studied art in Philadelphia, New York, and Europe. He created many paintings of early American historical figures both while living in Europe and America. He became famous for his paintings of American historical scenes. His works are filled with emotion and heroism.

MAKE A DRAWING FROM IMAGINATION! Although the painting, *Washington Crossing the Delaware* looks very realistic, it was not drawn or painted as the event was happening. When General George Washington crossed the Delaware River, it was a secret mission. The artist painted the scene much later from his imagination and from looking at people who posed for him. It is what he thought the event must have looked like. Draw a scene from your imagination. When drawing, hold the pencil as you would for writing. Hold the paper still with your other hand. Place lines on paper to FILL UP THE SPACE!

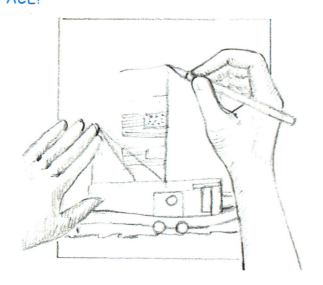

THE TIMES: Perhaps you already know that those who created the growing colonies came to America by ship from Europe. They wanted to dress like, make art like, and expand their territory just like the British. When the British King put restrictions on how far they could travel within this new continent, added taxes, and then sent British troops into their homes to keep watch, many decided that it was time to gain their freedom. The American Revolution began. It was a long and difficult war and the colonists had to create their first army. General George Washington did many courageous and daring maneuvers to gain victories during the war. This painting shows how he led the American troops in a surprise attack on Christmas Eve in 1776. The painting by Emanuel Leutze is more than 12 feet high and 21 feet long. The enormous size tells us this is an important man and an important event. For many years after the war, American artists were busy painting and sculpting the new American heroes in patriotic scenes, just as the British had created for their hero's and kings for centuries. Patriotic artwork gave people a sense of loyalty to the new nation and a sense of pride.

How to Set Up and Draw   Lesson 3

Techniques

Draw on a table, or a drawing board with a smooth surface, so that no texture is transferred through the paper. Carry the drawing board to any place you want to draw.

Working from a Photograph

When drawing from a photograph or picture, place the picture on the tabletop or drawing board beside the drawing paper. Attach the photograph or picture to the tabletop or drawing board with a binder clip or tape.

Working from an Object

When drawing an object, place the object on a table directly in front of you. Rest the drawing board on the edge of the table and your lap. This makes an easy angle to draw on. Sit far enough from the table that you can see the object clearly over the board. Keep an extra pencil, pencil sharpener, and eraser on the table within easy reach.

What to Look At

A good place to start a drawing is to draw the edges. The outside edge tells a lot about the object. To draw this silly frog figure we look at the edge. Start drawing at the bottom edge and follow that edge up and around the whole figure. Lines will curve where the object curves.

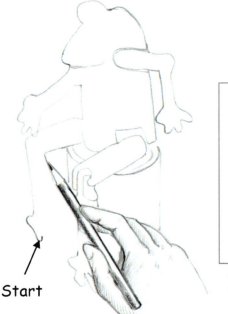
Start

Nicholas finds edges of different plastic animal figures in the drawing above.

SOMETHING TO TRY: Gather group of similar objects with different shapes. Your group could be plastic animals, cups from the kitchen, or figures from a collection within your home. Set the objects in front of you, above your drawing paper. Draw the outside edges of each object.

Draw a picture of a favorite subject. Draw all the lines and shapes you see while looking carefully at the object. See the reference list on the right to get ideas for subject matter. Remember to turn the paper in the correct position before starting.

Final Project Lesson 4

Application

Student Gallery

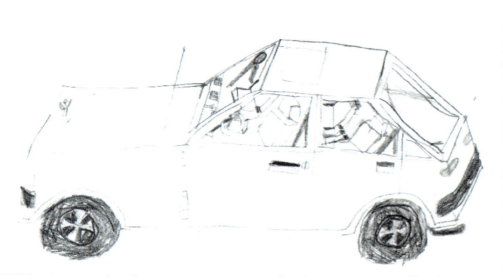

Student work by Matthew Ichiyasu shows detail outside and inside the car. The paper is placed in the horizontal position to best fit the shape of the car.

What are Media?

Media are the materials used to make art. Pencil, charcoal, and pastel are all drawing media. This book will introduce you to the media of pencil and markers. The medium and tools are listed here.

What is a Reference?

A reference is something we look at and draw from. It can be another work of art, a photograph, or a real life object. An object from life might be a chair, person, apple, or any other thing an artist sees. Reference suggestions are made for each project so that you become familiar with all the possibilities.

LOOK BACK! Did you consider how the position of the paper would fit the subject before beginning to draw? Did you choose a vertical or horizontal space in which to draw your subject?

YOU WILL NEED

- Drawing pencil
- Vinyl eraser
- Drawing paper
- Drawing board
- Pencil sharpener

REFER TO THE FOLLOWING WHEN DRAWING

Get your ideas from real objects, such as:
- a collection of robots
- car models
- doll figures
- toys

UNIT 2 line and shape Lesson 1

Vocabulary and Creative Exercise

Artists draw **lines** within a space to create a picture. A **shape** is made when both ends of a line connect. A shape can follow the outside edge of an object.

LINES

SHAPE

Explore Your World! A CREATIVE EXERCISE USING REAL-WORLD EXPERIENCE

Every time you step out the door, you have an opportunity to see objects in a new way. One part of your brain gives names to those objects and thinks about them in simple ways for easy identification. Using this part of your brain, you can identify the objects in the first row as a fish, a tree, and a bird. However, making art is more than identifying objects.

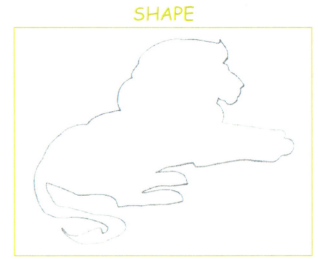

When studying art you will begin to use your visual brain. Your visual brain will notice more complicated shapes and lines when you look at familiar objects. The objects may look more like the images below than those above. TRY IT! Draw an object by looking at it and notice the details. Use lines that describe the object in more detail.

OBJECTIVE: to begin to see details and add lines that describes the object visually, rather than a shorthand method of depicting an object.

11

Looking at Line and Shape in Art   Lesson 2

Art nearly always begins with lines. Lines that show edges are called outlines. In this painting a line shows where the hills stop and the sky starts. Lines show the rough terrain of the hills and deep ridges of the plowed land. Lines sometimes show us directions. The broad lines in the blanket or shawl show us how it is wrapped around the man. We can use lines to show shapes like the face, hair, and pink shirt. Artists usually draw lines onto the picture, and then fill in the lines with color. Lines are redrawn and repainted as needed.

Oscar E. Berninghaus, *Indian Farmer*, 1926.
Photo Credit: Dover Publications Inc.

Lines show the outside edge of the hills.

Lines show the interior of the hill.

Lines show shapes of hand, face, hair, and shirt.

Thick lines show the direction of the shawl as it hangs off of the man's shoulders.

Lines show the curve of the road.

THE ARTIST:
Oscar Edmund Berninghaus (1874-1952)
American artist

Oscar E. Berninghaus is known for his paintings of Native Americans, New Mexico, and the American Southwest. Oscar was born in Saint Louis, Missouri beside the great Mississippi River. His father was a lithographer, a man who made art prints for people. The town of Saint Louis was the place that travelers stocked up on supplies before heading to the wild Western regions of the United States. This gave Oscar an opportunity to hear exciting stories about unsettled areas in the West. He was drawn to the life of the cowboys and especially was interested in the people who originally lived on the land. Native Americans became a theme in his paintings. He painted them realistically. He set the figures within their native surroundings of beautiful sage covered hills.

MAKE AN OBSERVATION DRAWING!
We often think about drawing each object in a scene. Sometimes we do not notice how all the objects fit together. In this drawing, step back and take a wider view showing what objects are in the surroundings.

Student work by Matthew Ichiyasu shows lines and shapes in a scene that includes what is around the train.

THE TIMES:
The land that European Americans began to inhabit was already inhabited by Native Americans. Many of those communities did not build permanent structures to live in, but the Pueblo people in the Southwestern part of the United States did. Pueblo is the name given to the people who inhabit the area and to their apartment-like buildings made of adobe mud and stone. The buildings surround an open space called a plaza. Bread is baked outdoors in adobe dome shaped ovens. The Taos Pueblo near the town of Taos, New Mexico has inhabited people for over 1,000 years, making it the oldest continually inhabited community in the United States. It is now inhabited by 150 residents who open part of it to tourists. There you can talk to artists, see traditional arts and crafts, taste the local food baked in outdoor ovens, and step into ancient pueblos. Over 5,000 Pueblo people live in separate homes adjacent to the Pueblo on nearly 50,000 acres of mountain land. In the early 1900's Americans were attracted to the Taos area. Six men, including Sharp, Couse, Berninghaus, Dunton, Blumenschein and Phillips, formed the Taos Society of Artists in 1915. Artists were attracted by the landscape and the people. These artists held traveling exhibits of their art across the United States. Critics said the colors were too bright and scenes too idyllic, but the artists claimed that they were painting the landscape and its people as they really are seen. The elevation and dry climate make colors appear vibrant. You can visit New Mexico today and see the same brilliant blue sky that these artists captured in their paintings. Berninghaus and his friends are among the most famous painters of the American West.

Art History

How to Draw Any Subject — Lesson 3

Techniques

What is Subject Matter?

Subject matter is the object of a picture. Subjects are often divided into categories like portrait, landscape, still life, animal, machine, and so on. In this book, you will use a variety of subjects. Always choose subjects that you like within the categories suggested.

When you begin to draw, take time to study the subject you've chosen. Turn the paper vertically or horizontally to fit the object or scene you wish to draw. As you draw, allow your hand to move around the paper. Do not rest your hand in one spot and expect your fingers to do all the moving. That would make the muscles in your fingers very tired!

1. Draw light outlines to make sure every object will fit on the page.

2. Redraw lines as needed, and then erase lines you don't want.

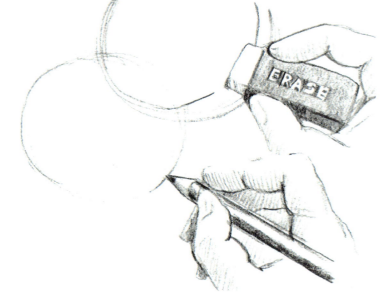

3. Draw lines inside the object and improve the outline.

4. Add the details.

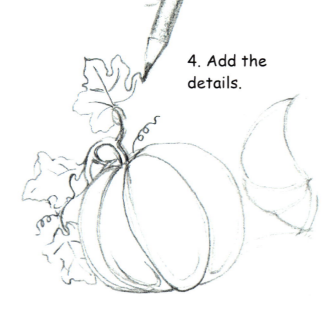

SOMETHING TO TRY: Find a subject from your toys or models. Spend time looking at the object to observe the direction of the lines and details before you begin to draw. Then draw the subject as you follow the instructions on this page. Don't worry about mistakes. Keep drawing and erase as needed.

Arrange a variety of fruits or vegetables on a table. Look for lines and shapes in the grouping of fruit or vegetables. Draw lines that show what is around the objects. What you see may look complex at first, but think about how you will simplify it into lines and shapes. Look carefully at the DIRECTION OF THE LINES. In the example shown, the lines we see on a pumpkin are not straight, but curve.

Final Project Lesson 4

Application

Common Mistake	What You Really See

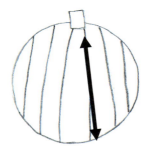 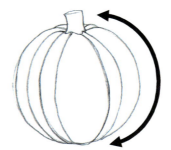

YOU WILL NEED

- Drawing pencil
- Vinyl eraser
- Drawing paper
- Pencil sharpener
- Drawing board

REFER TO THE FOLLOWING WHEN DRAWING

Use real or plastic fruit from your home or shop for some great shapes at the grocery store.

Use real or plastic vegetables in a variety of shapes.

Student Gallery

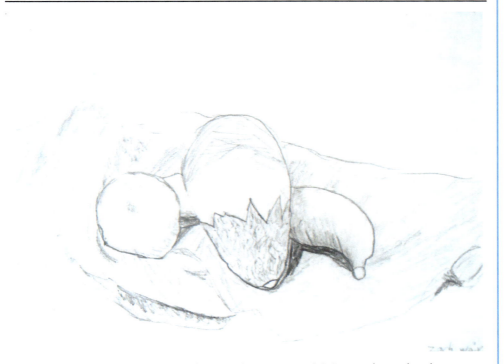

This group shows a banana, eggplant, and orange. Zack Weir outlines the shapes using lines that are dark enough to stand out from the paper. He draws lines to show the cloth. He uses dark lines in the center of the picture and light lines at the edges. This technique helps us focus on the center of the picture.

LOOK BACK! Did you show the different shapes of the fruit or vegetables by using lines? Did you use lines to show a cloth or table surface?

UNIT 3 — texture — Lesson 1

Vocabulary and Creative Exercise

Texture describes the surface of the object.
Textures can be: bumpy   rough   smooth   and more!

Explore Your World! A CREATIVE EXERCISE USING REAL-WORLD EXPERIENCE

Art is an opportunity to use all of your senses. Many people rush through the day without taking time to experience what is around them. Artists stop to watch the sun set or to feel the texture of a leaf. Making art helps artists to be more sensitive to what they see, feel, taste, and experience. When artists become more sensitive to touch and texture, they are able to draw these things. Make art to become more aware of what you see.

TRY IT: Take a blind walk. A partner is needed for this activity. Have your partner place a blindfold over your eyes. With the partner as your guide, follow. The partner should hold your hands and place them onto different textures. Touch as many different kinds of textures as possible. This is a good activity for outdoors but can be done indoors as well. When finished, look at the textures you touched. Draw some of the objects. You will be drawing from observation, but because you've taken the time to touch, you will be more aware of the surface of what you see.

OBJECTIVE: to develop sensory awareness, aiding in the ability to draw textured objects.

Looking at Texture in Art   Lesson 2

Textures can make a scene look more real. When looking at this painting you can imagine how the surfaces of tree bark, leaves, rocks, and grasses feel. This work by Asher B. Durand uses a variety of textures to portray the lush beauty found in nature.

Asher B. Durand (1796-1886),
Kindred Spirits, 1849
Photo Credit:
Dover Publications Inc.

Look at how the textures of these painted surfaces could be drawn in pencil, below.

THE ARTIST:
Asher B. Durand (1796-1886)
American Landscape Painter

Like many artists of his time, Durand was first trained as an etcher. The etching process uses lines and tonal values to produce an image. Detail is important. Durand was fascinated with textured details of trees and masses of foliage. He used these details in his paintings. He believed that students should be outdoors looking at nature to paint, rather than working indoors while learning techniques from the masters. Durand was a "constant supporter of younger artists, generous with advice and encouragement" (McLanathan 249).

MAKE AN OBSERVATION DRAWING! Do you have a spot of wilderness that you can walk through? Many cities have parks and walking trails. Observe nature like the American landscape artists did, and then sketch a scene on location. Draw some textures in your sketch.

Dots make texture. Move your pencil in a tiny circle to make a dot. Make them big, small, light or dark.

THE TIMES:
Native American cultures preserved the natural American landscape. Their way of life did not disturb or reshape the land. In the 1800's the American West remained an untamed wilderness. In 1803, the United States purchased the Louisiana Territory from France. This land deal doubled the size of the United States and the westward expansion began. As explorers and settlers traveled west, they were awed by valleys, natural streams, waterfalls, and a vast variety of wildlife. Large mountains seemed to stretch upward to the heavens and trees spread out to the horizon in every direction. These sites inspired the Hudson River School painters. Artists like Thomas Cole, Albert Bierstadt, Asher Durand, and others soon became the heroes of the time as they brought back views of this vast new land to an eager audience in the east. "The landscape tradition brought an elevated status to artists, essentially because of the religious connotations of the subject matter" (Wright 40). Many of these artists recognized God as the creator of such magnificent sights and felt they had a moral duty to make the sites visible to those who could not travel to see the sites first hand. Thomas Cole, who arrived in America at age seventeen, walked daily in the wild forests and fields with a sketchbook and flute in hand. He wrote, "creation!... all creation, lad... and none know how often the hand of God is seen in the wilderness, but them that rove it..." (McLanathan 239). Americans were so fascinated by the beauty of the land that they preserved many areas as national parks.

How to Make a Variety of Textures   Lesson 3

Techniques

Make textures by using different types of marks with the pencil. There is no specific mark that is right to use for a specific subject. It is up to the artist to decide what marks to use. Look at some different ways to make textures shown below.

LINES: Hold the pencil as you do when writing. This allows you to use the point. Make short, parallel strokes.

COMBINING SHAPES: Repeat any shape to form a group of shapes and make a texture.

COMBINING GROUPS OF LINES: Hold the pencil under your hand, using the side of the pencil lead. Drag the side of the pencil from one point to another. Lighten the pressure on the pencil as you near the end of the line.

BLENDING: Hold the pencil under your hand as shown using the side of the pencil lead. Use a back and forth motion with even pressure. Make a wide line that blends with others, creating a solid area.

SOMETHING TO TRY: Draw several objects found outdoors. Use different types of marks to show the textures. Try textures shown on this page or make up unique ones of your own.

Gather drawing tools. Attach paper to a drawing board using the clip at the top. If your board has a rubber band, put it around the bottom of the board and slip it over the bottom edge of your paper. This will hold the paper in place on windy days. Sit in a comfortable spot that is not in direct sunlight. Draw a view that has different textures in it. Show these textures in the drawing by making different types of marks.

Final Project Lesson 4

Application

Student Gallery

Student work by Erin Craven uses different marks for grass, the evergreen bush, and the stone path. The student uses dark pencil marks so the trees are easily visible. This scene was observed from her aunt's backyard.

YOU WILL NEED

- Drawing pencil
- Vinyl eraser
- Drawing paper
- Drawing board
- Pencil sharpener

REFER TO THE FOLLOWING WHEN DRAWING

An outdoor scene that you observed from one of the following places:
- A yard
- A park
- A field
- A sidewalk
- A window

LOOK BACK! Did you show texture by using a variety of lines or marks in the drawing? Point out the textures to your parent or teacher.

The Elements Combined: Line, Shape, and Texture

This additional lesson shows how you might use line, shape, and texture together in a picture. These techniques can be used with any subject. Choose your own subject and follow the steps on this page.

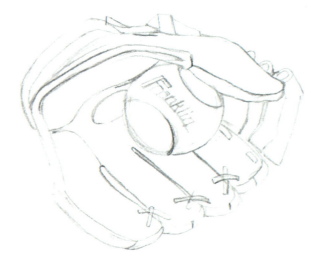

With lines, draw the basic shapes of the object. Here a ball rests within the mitt.

If you like the basic shapes of the objects, begin to add more details. Refine the outside edges. Erase extra lines.

You will spend the longest amount of time on the last step. Add marks that show the textures of what you see. Here dots are used in some parts of the glove and ball. Small connecting circles are seen in other areas. Dark marks, made with the Ebony pencil, help to define the edges.

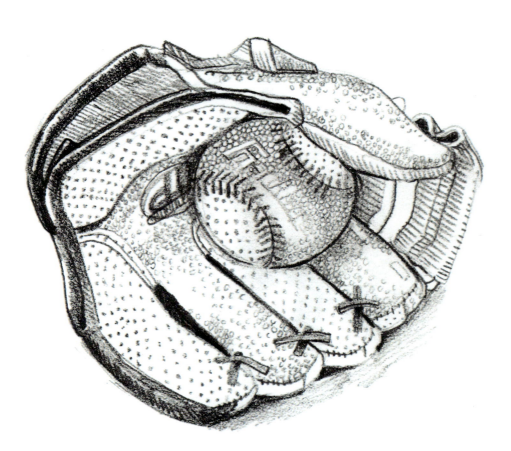

UNIT 4      Lesson 1

Value is how light or dark something appears when compared to a value scale. A value scale is shown below, from light to dark. The star appears to have different values on each side.

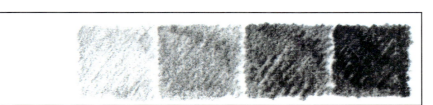

Explore Your World! A CREATIVE EXERCISE USING REAL-WORLD EXPERIENCE

Making art is an opportunity to experience the world differently. One naturally takes more time when looking at objects. This closer look is called observation. Artists who practice observing things in the natural world improve their ability to see! The more they see, the more they experience the world. Why make art? Make art in response to the world you see and experience.

TRY IT: Use a magnifying glass to reveal new sights of common objects in nature. Discover something new that you have not noticed about an object before. Draw this discovery on a piece of paper. After drawing the shape, add darker value around the edges to make the object stand out. Draw right up to the edge of the shape as shown.

NOTE: If you do not have a magnifying glass, use a mirror. Seeing a reflection of a thing can be eye opening as well.

OBJECTIVE: to notice the unique features of objects and to develop awareness of shape. Adding a dark value around the edges makes students more aware of those edges.

Looking at Value in Art   Lesson 2

When you draw a line, it is dark compared to the white of the paper. Dark stands out against light. This contrast makes the drawing pleasing to the eye. A drawing made of light lines is not as pleasant to look at because the lines do not contrast enough with the white of the paper. In Frederic Remington's painting, the values are clearly seen. The black horse, the black shirt, and the black clothing of the fallen man stand out from the light, sun-drenched prairie and sky.

Frederic Remington (1861-1909), *Aiding a Comrade*, c. 1890. Photo Credit: Dover Publications Inc.

It is easiest to see values clearly when looking at a gray image like the one on the right.

The lightest value is seen in the dust surrounding the fallen cowboy.

The sky and sundrenched landscape are a middle value.

The horses are a bit darker in value than the landscape that surrounds them.

The artist uses the darkest values in a triangle that draws our eyes to the action.

Art History

THE ARTIST:
Frederic Remington (1861-1909)
American Cowboy Artist

Frederic Remington is best known for his action-filled paintings of cowboys and Indians. He loved horses and outdoor life as a boy. He drew Western characters and battle scenes, though he was not a cowboy himself. He lived in the state of New York and had to make trips to the West, which he did often. There he gathered information for his pictures. He also made small-scale bronze sculptures of broncobusters.

MAKE AN OBSERVATION DRAWING!
It takes practice to draw solid areas of value. To get solid areas of value, draw simple shapes and fill them in. Keep the pressure on the pencil the same. Keep it lighter for light values. Keep it heavier for dark values. To make it fun, always choose shapes of things you like!

THE TIMES: Young men knew how to handle a gun and how to ride a horse after their involvement in the Civil War in the mid 1800's, so becoming a cowboy seemed like a good way to continue the kind of life they'd become used to. After the war, there was a need for beef in the more populated Eastern United States. Texas had cattle roaming free. America needed people to round up the cattle and drive them from Texas to railroad depots in Missouri, where the cattle could then travel by train to the Eastern states. Men doing the job were called cowboys. Cowboys endured the harsh climate of the southwest and made camp outdoors each night alongside the cattle. White men, African Americans, Mexicans, and Native Americans became cowboys. Skirmishes with Native American tribes were still taking place at this time as shown in Frederic Remington's painting, *Aiding a Comrade*. Newspapers told exaggerated stories about the Wild West and people in both America and Europe loved hearing about the heroes and outlaws who lived out West. When movies and TV were developed, America returned to telling stories of the cowboys through those new mediums. Cowboy stories remained popular throughout the 1950's.

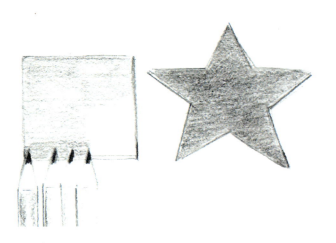

Value is created by using the side of the pencil as shown on page 19 and moving it back and forth. You can go over an area in different directions.

How to Add Value to a Drawing Lesson 3

To make a darker value, apply more pressure to the pencil. When applying dark values to the page, be careful not to smear the pencil marks with the side of your hand. Place a small piece of paper under your hand, resting on the paper instead of the drawing.

SOMETHING TO TRY: Make a value scale like the one shown on page 22. Draw five one-inch squares on drawing paper. Leave the first square white. Fill in the last square with the darkest mark the pencil allows. Draw the others as closely as possible to the values shown. Cut out your value scale.

1. Draw a picture in lines.

2. Add values to the picture. Look for light and dark by placing the value scale next to different areas. If drawing from real life, hold the scale in the air, overlapping the object, and decide which square it is most like. Once you decide which value to use, draw that value in your picture. Hold the value scale near the drawing if necessary, to see if it is dark enough. To make the darkest values, put more pressure on your pencil.

Draw first using line and shape to place the parts of the picture within the space of the page.

Add darks and grays using the value scale. Compare the values in the picture to the values in your value scale.

25

Student Gallery

Choose a photograph that shows light and dark values. Draw a picture of it, using both the lightest and darkest values. Use the value scale you made on page 25 to compare values in the photograph.

Artists are unique in the way they handled values. Look at the values in your reference photo when planning how you will use value.

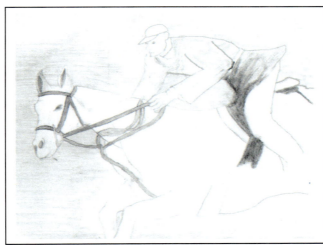

Above, Kendal Dehnart uses different values in the lines she drew. Lines showing the edges of the horse and his rigging are dark and heavy, while lines showing the edges of the man are light.

In the middle work, Jared Baughn uses light, middle, and dark values.

Ariel Ellis, in the work at right, makes a dark value in the background. This makes the ballerina stand out.

Final Project Lesson 4

Application

YOU WILL NEED

- Drawing pencil
- Vinyl eraser
- Drawing paper
- Drawing board
- Pencil sharpener

REFER TO THE FOLLOWING WHEN DRAWING

Find a book on a favorite subject that includes good photographs. Subjects could be:
- Sharks
- Space flight
- Trucks
- Ballet

LOOK BACK! Did you find a photograph of something you enjoy? Were light and dark values used in the drawing?

UNIT 5 — form — Lesson 1

Vocabulary and Creative Exercise

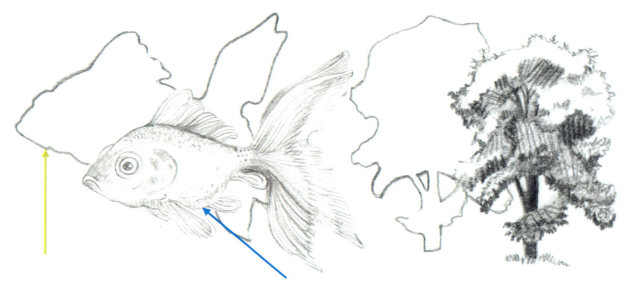

Shape is the outside edge or outline of an object. A shape is flat like a piece of cardboard. A shape is often more complex than simple circles and squares.

Form shows the object's roundness or depth. Form does not appear to be flat. Form is made by drawing inside the shape.

Which tree shows shape? Which tree shows form?

Explore Your World! A CREATIVE EXERCISE USING REAL-WORLD EXPERIENCE

Scientists take interest in what they find in the world. Artists do too. Science and art both use careful observation of the world as the beginning point for what they do. Art is sometimes made as a record of nature for scientific study. We all have a fascination for the design of nature once we have really taken a good look at what is there.

TRY IT: Choose a subject that is easy for you to find and explore. It could be leaves, seeds, flowers, stones, shells, or insects. Within that group, find at least five variations in shape. Draw each of the five objects near its actual size, showing the differences in size and shape. Do not trace around the objects! Draw the outline of each object freehand, while your eyes look at the object, then at the drawing and back and forth repeatedly.

OBJECTIVE: to gain greater visual awareness of shape and size and to develop observation skills and eye/hand coordination.

Looking at Form in Art   Lesson 2

Art Appreciation

Form shows the roundness of an object. Showing roundness or depth makes the objects appear more real. Artists do this by drawing lines that curve or by adding values that follow the surface. James Audubon draws the outline of the birds and the stump. He darkens the areas where there is an absence of light. He uses soft, blurred edges to show the curve of the owls' bodies. Audubon insisted on painting the birds life-size. Large birds were sometimes shown in awkward poses so that he could fit them on the paper.

John J. Audubon (1780-1851), *Snowy Owl*, from *Birds of America*. Photo Credit: Dover Publications Inc., NY.

The source of light is shinning from the upper left corner.

Light does not reach the right side and the underside of the tree branch.

Light does not reach the right side of the birds.

The use of smooth shading from dark to light creates a look of roundness or form on the owls' bodies and heads.

28

Art History

THE ARTIST:
James Audubon (1785-1851)
American Nature Explorer and Artist

James Audubon spent his boyhood days exploring the countryside of France. He collected birds' nests and made drawings of birds. Later he found the American wilderness even more exciting. He was the first to record the birds and animals of North America. He traveled along the Atlantic coast, as well as the Ohio, Mississippi, and Missouri Rivers. He brought only a gun, flute, art supplies, and his dog. He spent an average of seventeen hours each day making art, and saw exciting things like alligator battles and sea turtles depositing eggs in the sandy beaches. He spent his lifetime painting in the wilderness areas, and traveling to raise funds for the production of his *The Birds of America, Ornithological Biography,* and *The Viviparous Quadrupeds of North America,* all with many volumes and produced in large colorful formats.

THE TIMES:
The early explorers of the North American continent found that it was wider and stretched out further than anyone would have guessed possible. Its vast variety of plants, animals, and birds seemed endless. Delightful new discoveries of wildlife, not found in Europe, could be made every day. Early American naturalists were eager to document all of them. One of the first naturalists was John Bartum. Born in 1699, he was a hard working Quaker and farmer in the Colonial period. He tells of a day when, weary from holding the plough, he sat down to rest and noticed a daisy. His curiosity was aroused. He purchased a book on plants and a book on Latin grammar so that he could read the text. Bartum then studied for three months with a neighboring schoolmaster to learn to read Latin (McLanathan 217). He became one of the most famous botanists of the time, supplying plants to gardens, parks, and estates in Europe and America. Alexander Wilson learned to draw and paint from Bartum's son and produced eight volumes of *American Ornithology,* books on the birds of North America. Bird lovers everywhere sent him specimens and information from their own observations for his project (McLanathan 218). John James Audubon adventured even further into the American continent to paint the birds, small animals, and plant life.

MAKE AN OBSERVATION DRAWING! Artists sometimes copy in order to study how another artist works. John Bartum taught his son to paint the things he saw and he taught his friend, Alexander Wilson. You can learn from these men too. The purpose of a copy is not to make an exact reproduction, but to learn from what you see. Draw a simple outline of Audubon's painting on the previous page. Look at the shapes of the birds and which direction their bodies curve. Draw lines that curve in those directions.

How to Show Form Lesson 3

Techniques

Line can do more than show the outline or shape as seen in sample #1. Lines can show the form or thickness of an object. To do this the line should follow the direction of the surface. The lines curve around a rounded object as shown in sample #2. Another way to show form is to soften the edges of a shape by blending with a pencil. Use the side of the pencil and follow an edge making it dark, then blending or softening the area as it curves around the object as shown in sample #3.

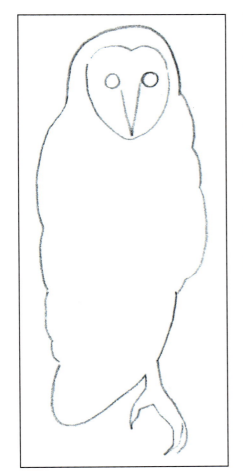

#1 SHAPE   #2 FORM WITH LINE   #3 FORM WITH SOFT EDGE

SOMETHING TO TRY: Choose a simple object. It is easier to see form in a real object than in a photograph of an object. Draw the surfaces you see by using either lines or shading to show form. These surfaces have different directions so the lines should flow in those directions. Make marks throughout the shape to show form.

30

Birds are interesting because of the variety of shapes and form. When drawing from real life, choose a bird that stays in sight awhile.
- Gulls tend to pause for long periods.
- Ducks or geese stand in one position as they peck the ground for food.
- Woodpeckers move busily, but do not fly away unless startled.
- Pigeons make good models.

Quietly and slowly take your place beside a bird or observe from a window. Next, quickly draw its shape. Then draw lines to show its form. Add details. If the bird moves at this point, you can continue to add details. Alternatively, you may draw from still models if you have access to stuffed birds in a taxidermist shop, a Natural History Museum, or a large sporting goods store with animal models.

Student Gallery

Student work above is by Heidi Grogan. Notice how the artist drew into the shape to show form and into the background to make the drawing interesting.

LOOK BACK! Does the drawing show the form of the bird as well as the shape?

Final Project
Lesson 4

YOU WILL NEED

- Drawing pencil
- Vinyl eraser
- Drawing paper
- Drawing board
- Binder clips
- Pencil sharpener

REFER TO THE FOLLOWING WHEN DRAWING

- A real bird observed from outdoors or a window
- A model of a bird
- A caged pet bird

UNIT 6 form using value Lesson 1

Vocabulary and Creative Exercise

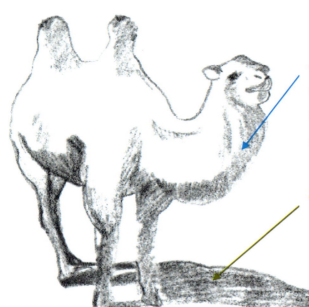

Shading helps show the **form** of an object. One way to shade is to blend using the side of the pencil lead, creating a smooth area of value.

Shadow is seen when light is blocked.

Explore Your World! A CREATIVE EXERCISE USING REAL-WORLD EXPERIENCE

Artists often draw more than an outline. They want the object to look real so the viewer can experience it on paper in a similar way that the artist experienced it in real life. To do this the artist shades areas of the drawing to show light and dark sides.

TRY IT: Draw the outline of a small, folded paper sack by tracing around its four sides. What shape do you see? Now open the sack and set it on a table in front of you. You may want to crumple it a bit for added interest. Draw what you see on another sheet of paper. There more to draw than only the four lines, as in the first drawing. Draw the dark and light areas using shading. See page thirty-four for an example of this type of drawing.

Note: If a paper sack is not available, the project can be done with a small box or other simple item.

OBJECTIVE: to discover the difference between shape and form while inventing ways of showing those differences on paper.

Looking at Shading and Shadow in Art   Lesson 2

Art Appreciation

We can see form when light shines on an object. The dark area is shaded. In this painting by Charles Peale, the arms and legs look rounded. The light appears to be shinning from the left side as if it comes from a window. Shading is seen on the white stockings of the lower figure. Shadows are seen on the wall behind the figure and on the steps. These are made when light is blocked by the figure.

Within this one section of the painting, we see all the parts that make up a picture using light, shading, and shadows.

The lightest area of the green wall shows the direction the light comes from. Light shines from the center left of the picture. The right side is darker.

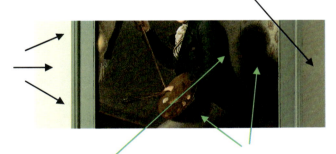

Shading is shown on the right of objects such as the sleeve, opposite the direction from which the light is shining.

Shadows are thrown onto surfaces behind the object. The boy's shadow is seen on the wall. The paint palette shadow is seen on the leg of his trousers.

Look for other shadows and shaded areas in this painting.

Charles Wilson Peale (1741-1827) *The Staircase Group*. 1795. Oil on canvas. 89 x 39 ½ ". Photo Credit: Dover Publications Inc., NY.

THE ARTIST:
Charles Wilson Peale (1741-1827) Artist, Revolutionary Soldier, Naturalist, and Scientist.

Charles Wilson Peale is widely considered the most extraordinary man in the history of American art. He was an enthusiastic, warmhearted, and imaginative man. As a colonist in America, Charles sided with the Sons of Liberty during the American Revolution. He lost his saddle making business because of his friendships with these Patriots. That did not stop Peale. "He was unusual in that, like Leonardo da Vinci, the great artist and scientist of the Renaissance, he was interested in all arts, all crafts, and all of nature" (Batterberry 64). He decided to become a painter and painted all of the American Revolutionary heroes as he worked along with them, as a soldier. A fellow soldier wrote, "He fit (fought) and painted, painted and fit (fought)" (Batterberry 64). After the war, his interests led him to become a naturalist, one who studies nature, and he created the first Natural History Museum in North America. His museum displayed wild life arranged in painted habitats, Indian relics, fossils, and mastodon bones, which he had helped to excavate. He taught his seventeen children to paint and named many after famous Renaissance artists such as Raphael, Titian, Rembrandt, and Rubens.

MAKE AN OBSERVATION DRAWING!
Place a cup, glass, or similar still life object in front of you. Allow light to shine onto it from one side. First, fill the object in with the value of the object. Then, darken the shaded areas. Lighten the highlights with an eraser.

THE TIMES:
Not all the colonists wanted freedom from Britain and King George III's laws that dictated how they should be ruled. They felt that government systems had always included kings, emperors, or pharaohs, all with absolute power over the people they ruled. However, the American colonies were founded by people from all over Europe who had been punished for their religious beliefs and wanted to make their own rules to live by. Pilgrims, Puritans, Catholics and Quakers from England, Jews from Spain and Portugal, and Dutch all left Europe to obtain freedom to practice their own religions and set up their own laws. While some remained loyal to their European heritage, many did not like the new laws that the king had made. New ideas of independence circulated throughout the colonies by men like Thomas Paine in his pamphlet, *Common Sense*, where he wrote, "For as in absolute governments the King is law, so in free countries the law *ought* to be King". Thomas Jefferson wrote in the Declaration of Independence that men are created equal, that they are given or "endowed by their Creator with certain unalienable rights that among these are Life, Liberty and the pursuit of Happiness." These publications helped people understand why their freedom was worth fighting for. Americans continue to fight for freedom of religion and speech within our own government because there will always be those who want to take those rights away. Voting is one way citizens of America make their opinions heard.

How to See Shading and Shadow   Lesson 3

Using Only One Light Source

A light source is the source from which light is shining. An object seen indoors might have many light sources from lamps, multiple windows, or lights from other rooms. The clearest way to see form is to use one source of light. A single window is a perfect source. Other sources should be controlled by shutting off lights and closing curtains and shades.

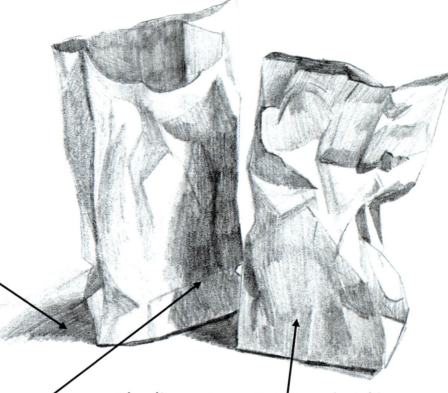

Shadows occur when objects block the light. Drawing the surface that the object sits on, even if it is only a part of that surface, gives more reality to the drawing. If some indication of surface is not drawn, the object looks like it floats in empty space. Many times simply drawing the shadow is enough to imply a surface.

Shadow occurs on other surfaces where an object blocks light, as shown in this area.

Shading makes a flat shape look like a rounded, thick form. The thickness is seen because of light and dark areas. Shading occurs on the object where light is blocked. Shading can be shown using blending techniques that are shown on page nineteen.

SOMETHING TO TRY: Look outdoors for objects that have form. Trees, buildings, pots, or boulders have form. Make sure that the form is clearly seen. Draw one object showing form by shading. Draw any shadows you observe.

Set up a still-life using one source of light. Arrange two objects side by side. Draw shapes first as you place the lines on paper to fill the page. Make needed corrections as you work. Add shading to show form once you like where things are placed on the space of the page. Use shadow to connect the objects visually to the surface of the table.

Final Project Lesson 4

Application

Student Gallery

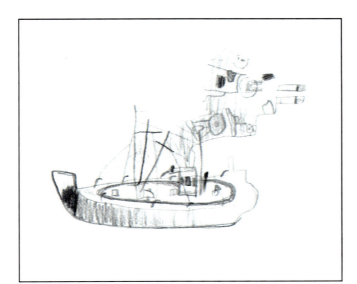

Student work by Aaron Garrison shows a model boat and Star Wars fighter.

Student work by Ariel Ellis shows a flowerpot and ceramic figure.

Both works show shading on the objects and shadow on the surface of the table.

YOU WILL NEED

- Drawing pencil
- Vinyl eraser
- Drawing paper
- Drawing board
- Pencil sharpener

REFER TO THE FOLLOWING WHEN DRAWING

Find two objects that appeal to you. They may be found in your room, the kitchen cabinets, on a knick-knack shelf, or in a collection. Choose objects that stand up. Do not choose flat objects like books or silverware.

LOOK BACK! Did you use shading to show the form of the objects in your drawing? Did you use shadows to show the surface they were sitting on?

UNIT 7 — local value — Lesson 1

Vocabulary and Creative Exercise

Local Value is the lightness or darkness of the object that is determined by its natural color.

Light local value Middle local value Dark local value

Explore Your World! A CREATIVE EXERCISE USING REAL-WORLD EXPERIENCE

Most places on the earth are pleasant to look at. This is usually why we love being outdoors. Walls block out nature's beauty. Therefore, people hang art on them. People have decorated their walls to bring the beauty of nature indoors for thousands of years. The beauty of seeing shape and form on paper is why people enjoy receiving art and surrounding themselves with it whether it is with pictures, greeting cards, or posters. Share your art with others. It is a way to communicate your thoughts and ideas.

TRY IT: Draw a picture to give to someone special. Draw a subject that they are fond of. If your sister likes horses, draw a picture of one for her. If your dad loves football, draw a picture of a football or his favorite player. Fill in the object with the correct value, either light value, middle value, or dark value. An object may have more than one value. Look closely!

OBJECTIVE: to experience a purpose for making art and the joy of sharing it with others and to notice the local value of the object.

Looking at Value and Light in Art   Lesson 2

Every object has local value that describes how light or dark it is. This man's suit is white, but the parts that are not directly in sunlight are of a middle value. Some parts of the suit are very dark in value. Learning to see values is one of the most important skills you will need as an artist.

Cecilia Beaux; *Man with the Cat*, 1898
Photo Credit: Dover Publications Inc.

Dark value, middle value, light value

We know the suit is off-white in color. The value changes depending how much light is directed on it.

The cat sits on the man's lap absorbing the sun's warmth. We see dark values inside the ears where sunlight does not reach.

We see light values where sun shines on the fur.

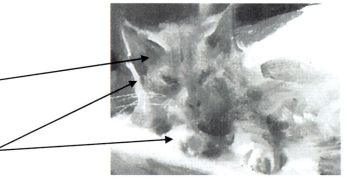

Art Appreciation

Art History

THE ARTIST:
Cecilia Beaux (1855-1942)
American Portrait Painter

Cecilia Beaux was considered the finest woman painter at the turn of the century. She was raised by an aunt who encouraged her to paint. She painted many portraits of important figures in America including Mrs. Theodore Roosevelt, wife of the 26th U.S. president. In 1895, Beaux became the first full-time woman faculty member at the Pennsylvania Academy of the Fine Arts. She taught drawing and painting. She was especially skilled in painting portraits.

THE TIMES:
In the 1800's many rights of American citizens did not apply to women. They could not vote and most states had laws limiting a woman's right to own property. Most colleges were closed to women. Susan B. Anthony and Elizabeth Cady Stanton helped found the National Woman Suffrage Association to help women gain the right to vote. Susan was arrested for casting a vote in the 1872 presidential election. Many people, including women, were opposed to women voting and working in high positions like Cecilia Beaux held as a college professor. Things began to change for women when, in 1920, the Nineteenth Amendment was added to the Constitution allowing women to vote.

MAKE AN OBSERVATION DRAWING! Draw three simple objects using local value only. Choose one light, one middle-gray, and one dark object. Next, add a source of light and make areas lighter with the eraser. Notice that the light area on the darkest value is not as light as the one on the lightest value.

As you fill in spaces with value, exert the same amount of pressure on the pencil and make your marks close together. Leaving white areas in between marks will confuse the eye.

How to Work with a Neutral Ground   Lesson 3

Techniques

Make the neutral ground about this dark.

Cover the paper with pencil. Rub it into the paper with a cotton ball to make a smooth, dark background.

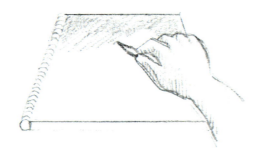

Draw the outline onto the neutral ground.

Lift out lighter areas with an eraser (shown on page 39).
Draw darker values into the areas you want darkest.

SOMETHING TO TRY: Work from a photograph that shows at least three different values. Choose an object that is more complex in shape than those in the previous lessons are. Draw a picture beginning with a neutral ground as shown above.

Light an object from only one side. Draw the object showing local value and the effect of light as it creates lighter and darker areas. Compare the object with the values you see around the object. Draw the background values.

Student Gallery

This work is by Amy Wright. The cup is lit from the back, which casts the shadow forward. The mark making in the background and on the surface of the table creates interest in the drawing.

Final Project Lesson 4

Application

YOU WILL NEED

- Drawing pencil
- Vinyl eraser
- Drawing paper
- Drawing board
- Pencil sharpener

REFER TO THE FOLLOWING WHEN DRAWING

Observe a real object. It could be a person, an inanimate object, or a pet.

LOOK BACK! Was the object positioned so that it had light from one side? Did you draw the effect of light as seen on the object and the background?

The Elements Combined: Values and Forms

This additional lesson shows how you might add values to show form in a picture. These techniques can be used with any subject. Choose your own subject and follow the steps on this page.

Shapes of the vegetables are drawn onto the page with lines. Hatch lines on the eggplant are started to suggest darker values and forms.

Two ways of showing form were used here. On the eggplant the dark and light values were blended. The suggestion of light on the top of the vegetable shows form. Dark and light lines are used on the artichoke. The direction of the line shows the form. The group of tomatoes on the left edge of the paper is filled in then lightened with an eraser. Darkest values are concentrated near the center of the page.

UNIT 8   contrast   Lesson 1

Vocabulary and Creative Exercise

You draw dark lines on a white background when you use a pencil on regular paper. Scratch-art is the opposite. White lines are scratched into a dark background. When the white is compared to the black, we notice the stark difference. We can say that the white lines contrast with the black of the page.

Explore Your World! A CREATIVE EXERCISE USING REAL-WORLD EXPERIENCE

We make art to gain a richer experience of our lives. Close your eyes. Listen! Experience the world through sound. You may never notice a train station in the background until you hear the train whistle. You may never think of putting birds in your drawing until you hear them all around you. You may never realize the force of a fire until you hear the crackling and popping of the wood it consumes. When you hear sounds, you can then focus on seeing what is causing the sounds. When we make art, we have a reason to observe these types of things more closely for the purpose of drawing them.

TRY IT: First, go outdoors. Close your eyes for about one minute and listen. Make a mental list of the things you hear. Take time to really enjoy this process of listening. Then open your eyes and draw a picture of the world you just experienced through sound. You can scratch the picture into a piece of scratch art paper or use pencil on paper.

OBJECTIVE: to use of the sense of hearing to aid in seeing.

Looking at Contrast in Art — Lesson 2

Folk Art is created by those who have no formal training. Americans created a lot of folk art early in the nation's history. The works are unique. Here the artist, Milton William Hopkins, paints a dark background and contrasts that with light areas. The young boy's clothing is dark like the background. His face, hands, and socks carry our eyes through the dark space. His dog is a large mass of light color and a very special part of this portrait of young Pierrepont Edward Lacey.

Milton William Hopkins, *Pierrepont Edward Lacey and His Dog, Gun,* 1832.
Photo Credit: Dover Publications Inc.

Here light and dark areas are reversed so that you can more clearly see the placement of the contrasting areas. Notice that contrasting areas are spaced from the top of the picture to the bottom.

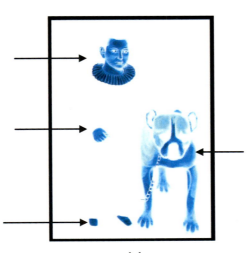

This is not just any dog, but a light colored dog. If the boy owned a black dog, would we be able to see it? The contrast of light against dark gets our attention. Here the darker blue color shows the areas of greatest contrast.

44

THE ARTIST:
Milton William Hopkins (1789-1844)
American Folk Artist

Hopkins was an early American itinerant artist. Business was good for artists who were willing to travel during this time of growth and movement within the new nation of the United States of America. Hopkins traveled to Albion, New York, one of the cities and towns that grew instantly after the Erie Canal was finished in 1825. He did many things there. He worked as a house painter, a sign painter, and a portrait painter. He also made chairs, was an auctioneer, and worked as a canal boat captain (D'Ambrosio).

THE TIMES:
There was little in the early stages of America to attract trained European artists, but the desire for art existed. To fill that need a sign painter would also be a portrait painter. Tombstone and ship carvers became sculptors (McLanathan 267). Some traveled throughout the new settlements. Others kept a shop. It was common for these self-trained artists to fill any need that arose in their small communities. Most of these self-made artists had never seen a painting from the European tradition and so there is great individuality and uniqueness in their works. We call it folk art.

SOMETHING TO TRY: You can look at negative space as well as the objects (positive space). Gather some fresh leaves. Lay them in a way that creates interesting negative space. Place a piece of paper over the group. Do a rubbing by using the side of the pencil lead. Use the entire lead to rub back and forth, like blending. Next, draw lines around the outside edges so they can be seen clearly. Then fill in the NEGATIVE space in a dark value for contrast.

negative space

How to Make Texture with Scratch Art Lesson 3

Work from a photograph of an animal with lots of texture so that you have many lines in the work. Draw an outline that shows the shape of the animal. Draw it large and fill the space.

Once an outline is completed, draw lines or marks to show textures. The white lines will contrast with the dark background. Take your time at this point in the work. Drawing many tiny lines really pays off. Here we show the types of marks used in the picture of the fox. Complete your picture.

Short scratches show medium length fur on its forehead.

Scratch tiny marks to show the short fur on its nose.

Leave the dark areas like eyes or nose black. Do not fill in as you would in a pencil drawing. Pay attention to what is white and what is black.

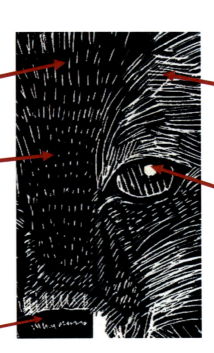

Scratch large lines in the direction of the fur at the side of its face.

Scratch out some areas completely so that very little black remains.

Once you have finished the animal, decide if scratching into the background is necessary. At times, a background could add interest. Other times it will distract from the animal.

Using the scratch art instructions, make a picture of a mammal, bird, or reptile that has texture in fur, feathers, or skin. You will need to observe details carefully so use a photograph. Calendar photos come in a large format showing lots of detail.

Final Project Lesson 4

Application

Student Gallery

Scratch-art is by Annie Marie Walker.

YOU WILL NEED

- Scratch-art paper
- Scratch stick

REFER TO THE FOLLOWING WHEN DRAWING

Use a photograph of a subject that has a lot of detail or texture. It may be:
- A bird
- An animal
- An insect

LOOK BACK! Did you fill up the page with the object? Did you draw more than just the outline by scratching in textures and filling in spaces?

UNIT 9 the shapes of natural forms   Lesson 1

Vocabulary and Creative Exercise

Shape is important because it is how people recognize objects. The shapes of geometric objects such as a peach or a ball may look the same no matter what angle we view them. The shapes of natural forms like people and animals can change a lot depending on what angle we see them.

Explore Your World! A CREATIVE EXERCISE USING REAL-WORLD EXPERIENCE

The normal activities that you do each day are good subjects to make art from. Brushing teeth, making the bed, or playing are subjects for art. Some activities involve more than one person in your household. Dad tickles someone or he teaches how to bait the fishing hook and cast the line. Mom serves a meal or ties a little brother's shoelaces. Think of common experiences and picture them in your mind. To picture something is to recall the image or to imagine. When Mom picks out a new carpet, she **imagines** how the new color will look in the room that she wants to put it in. Do this before putting your ideas on paper as well. When we draw in this way, we use what we've seen, what we've remembered, and some imagination. Our brains are really working!

TRY IT: Draw an experience that you have seen and that involves several family members. Draw it as you remember it. For a new experience, draw with a white pencil on black construction paper.

OBJECTIVE: to think of the common everyday experience as worthy subject matter for art and to recall visual images using memory, while inventing compositions.

Looking at Shapes in Art   Lesson 2

Art Appreciation

Every object has a shape. Complex shapes change as the object turns or is viewed from different sides. Some shapes tell us more about the object than others do. When we look at the three large animals in the painting below, the lion, the bear, and the bull, we recognize them by their shapes. As you look at the shapes, notice which direction the curved lines go in the legs, back, and rump of the animals. Seeing these curves will help you to draw animals.

Edward Hicks (1780-1849), *The Peaceable Kingdom*, c.1837.
Photo Credit: Dover Publications Inc.

The animal shapes are curved, like this bull's neck and back, giving a calm, peaceful feeling to the picture.

Because the lion is drawn from a side view, the shape tells us a lot about the animal. We see the arching back and curve of the tail. We see all four legs.

49

THE ARTIST:
Edward Hicks (1780-1849)
Colonial Quaker Artist

Edward Hicks is well known for his many interpretations of *The Peaceable Kingdom* where he placed young children alongside wild animals who pose like elegant statues. His paintings are based on the idea of peace as it is described in the Bible. Edward Hicks read in Isaiah 11:6 that the wolf will dwell with the lamb and a little child shall lead the creatures. Can you find the wolf and the lamb in the painting we just looked at? Often his paintings contain a middle scene of William Penn signing a treaty with Native Americans. Hicks earned his living painting houses and signs, and taught himself to paint pictures. In his paintings, he expressed the Quaker belief in peaceful coexistence.

MAKE AN OBSERVATION DRAWING: Draw an animal. Use any type of reference that you have available. Look for shapes inside the form of the animal. Begin by drawing those shapes. Add lines and watch the direction of the curves. Finish the animal with just line or draw form using lines within the shape. You can use the same steps shown here, when you use white pencil on black paper. You decide.

THE TIMES: A key event in Pennsylvania's history was the 1682 peaceable agreement between Pennsylvania's founder, William Penn and the Indians. Penn was admired by Native Americans because he traveled unarmed and he could run faster than most, which earned him great respect. He negotiated peacefully with the Susquehannocks, Shawnees, and Leni-Lenape tribes. He believed in the free practice of any religion, low taxes, private ownership of land, and many other freedoms that they had not had in Europe. Jim Powell states, "Liberty brought so many immigrants that by the American Revolution Pennsylvania had grown to some 300,000 people and became one of the largest colonies. Pennsylvania was America's first great melting pot."

Shapes and Lines

Finish with line.

Finish using form.

How to Best Show the Subject — Lesson 3

Techniques

Some angles create shapes that give more information about the subject. Explore the best angle to show the most information. Here are examples of poor angles and good angles. Poor angles show little information about the object. Good angles show lots of information about the object. Which angle is the best at describing the characteristics of a wolf?

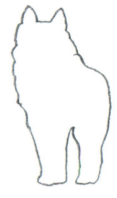  

POOR– This front view shows little of the face and legs. It could be a cat.

GOOD – More of the legs show, but the face and tail disappear at this angle.

BEST – Here each leg is separated so we see it as a four-legged animal. The tail stands away from the body so that it is clearly seen. The head is angled so we see the long snout.

If you look at the outside edge of the three animals below, you will notice that the shapes made by their bodies helps us identify them. They have unique shapes.

SOMETHING TO TRY: Draw the shape of one of the animals above. These are drawn with black marks on white paper, but you will draw with white pencil on black construction paper. Look carefully for the white areas within the shape. These areas are where you will make white marks with the white pencil.

Final Project Lesson 4

Application

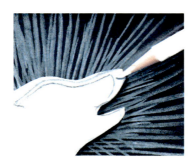

Draw an animal shape that clearly shows the characteristics of the animal. Fill up the paper. Cut out the shape. This cutout is your template. Place the paper cutout (template) on a black sheet of construction paper. With one hand, hold the template to the black paper. With the other hand, draw rays that start at the template and go out almost to the edge of the paper. Make lines that go from thick to thin by using pressure and then lessening the pressure as you draw each line.

YOU WILL NEED
- Drawing paper
- Black construction paper
- Scissors
- White colored pencil
- Colored pencils (optional)

REFER TO THE FOLLOWING WHEN DRAWING

Use a photograph of a subject that has a lot of detail and shows the object's recognizable shape. It may be:
- A bird
- An animal
- An insect

Student Gallery

Moriah Hanson cut templates for two deer, seen nose to nose. She adds colored grass and flowers.

LOOK BACK! Did you choose an angle that best shows the characteristics of the subject you chose? Is the subject identifiable to others?

UNIT 10   edges   Lesson 1

Vocabulary and Creative Exercise

An edge is a line or border at which a surface stops. The edges of a silhouette tell us so much about a person that we can often identify him. A silhouette is a representation of a person in profile showing only the outline against a contrasting background. This type of art is a perfect example of how important edges can be in art.

Explore Your World! A CREATIVE EXERCISE USING REAL-WORLD EXPERIENCE

Edges tell us a lot. When we look at things from different angles, the edges are different. Some angles tell us more information than others do. Look at a cup with the handle toward you. Now look at a cup with the handle to the side so that you can see its edge. If you wanted to show someone what the cup looked like by drawing only the edges, which angle would you choose? Ancient cultures were very aware of edges and used no shading to show shadows and form. They always chose to draw the face from the side so that they could see the person more clearly. You can see silhouettes in Egyptian and Mesopotamian art.

TRY IT: Ask a person to pose for a few minutes while you draw the outside edge of their face. First, have them face toward you as you draw the outside edge. Then have the person turn their face to the side so that the silhouette is seen. Draw the outside edge.

> OBJECTIVE: to think about edges and experience the type of edges that give the most information.

53

Looking at Edges in Art — Lesson 2

Augustin Edouart (1789-1861) *Martin Van Buren*. 05 Dec 1782-24 July 1862. Silhouette, 1841. Lithograph, chalk and cut paper on paper. 27.8x 21 cm. Gift of Robert L. McNeil, Jr. National Portrait Gallery, Smithsonian Institution, Washington, DC, U.S.A. Photo Credit: National Portrait Gallery, Smithsonian Institution/ Art Resource, NY

A type of art was brought to America from Europe that depended entirely on the edge to show a person's image. They found that the silhouette, or side view, gave the most information and many portraits like the one above were cut from dark paper, and then attached to a light paper. A background was sometimes drawn in as shown in the example above of a portrait of Martin Van Buren.

A silhouette shows the outside edge of the subject as shown in this line drawing.

The silhouette of Martin Van Buren tells us much about him. He stands upright with shoulders back, which lets us know that he is a confident man.

His clothing includes a vest, high-collared shirt, pants, new shoes, and a jacket. All of these were the latest style. This tells us that he is a well dressed man and held a high position in society.

THE ART: The black cutout silhouette was developed to take the place of miniature portraits. Only the wealthy could afford painted portrait miniatures. These were like oversized pins or worn on a chain like a necklace. The less wealthy, wanting a portable likeness of their loved ones, made silhouettes cut from paper. Early settlers to America, continuing this European tradition, filled albums with likenesses of their families and friends. Paper was affordable and a silhouette artist could earn a living by cutting it to look like a person.

MAKE AN OBSERVATION DRAWING!

Have someone sit in profile against an empty wall. You want to see the side of their face with no distractions in the background. Use an ebony pencil or a white pencil on black paper. Draw their profile as you see on page 53. Include part of the neck. Cut it out and attach it with a glue stick to a white sheet of drawing paper. You may want to complete many cutouts of this type. You could draw and cut out one of each family member just as the Americans in the 17th and 18th centuries did.

The miniature portrait above was painted by an American artist, Edward Green Malbone, in 1801. Its actual size is shown. It was painted with watercolor on ivory. It is a portrait of *Eliza Izard (Mrs. Thomas Pinckney Jr.)*. Photo Credit: Dover Publications Inc.

THE TIMES: Once America won its freedom from English rule, those who led the way became the new American heroes. Their portraits were painted by many artists from Great Britain, France, and Italy who had come to celebrate a new republic. Some painters were very decorative and others more realistic in style. Miniature portraits were only for those who could afford such luxuries. Most Americans could not. The foreign artists made such an impression that Americans everywhere wanted portraits of their family and loved ones in whatever manner they could afford. In the first half of the eighteenth century, before the camera was developed, portrait artists were in high demand and they traveled from town to town.

How to Draw with Marker   Lesson 3

Hold the marker lightly to the paper. Do not smash the end by pressing hard. Always put the cap back on when you're not using it, even when you are switching from one marker to another. Markers come in different widths. The width of the marker changes the way the line looks, giving different results.

FINE POINT

When drawing with only a fine point marker, use a variety of lines to make the drawing more interesting. Lines can be short, long, close together, far apart, straight, or curved. Lines can change direction. Look at the kinds of lines used in the drawing of a monkey. A fine point marker is appropriate for a delicate drawing of a small furry animal such as this.

BROAD POINT

The broad point marker is a way to add more variety to a drawing. The strokes are thick and heavy looking. When drawing with a broad point marker, vary the width of the line by changing the angle of the marker where it touches the paper. The drawing of the ocean liner is made with a broad, flat marker. The wide lines are appropriate for a massive machine like the ocean liner.

SOMETHING TO TRY: Find pictures of objects you like. Draw one of them using a fine point maker and another using a broad point marker.

Look at an object and draw it with white pencil from profile (side view). Cut it out. Glue the silhouette onto white paper showing the side without pencil marks. Add a background using your markers. A simple line drawing looks good with the dark silhouette.

Final Project Lesson 4

Application

Student Gallery

Student work by Roland Warns (at the right) shows a cut silhouette of a dog. He drew a background with a marker. Nicholas Warns cut out a ship and finished with a seascape background in marker (below).

YOU WILL NEED

- Black construction paper
- White paper
- Scissors
- Glue stick
- Black markers

REFER TO THE FOLLOWING WHEN DRAWING

Use a photograph of an animal, object, or person, which shows the object's shape in a way that identifies the object.

LOOK BACK! Did you look carefully at the outside edge as you cut or drew the shape? Are others able to identify what is in your silhouette?

COMPOSITION

Composition is about the arrangement and placement of either a group of objects or the different parts of one object. You will look at ideas of arrangement such as balance and rhythm. You can arrange the objects within a picture in many different ways. You will see how artists of the past have accomplished balance and rhythm within their picture spaces. Next, you will look at the techniques of overlapping and depth. You will also look at the parts that make up a human face and an animal's body. You will learn how to use the following ideas into your pictures.

BALANCE
RHYTHM
OVERLAP
DEPTH
PROPORTION OF THE FACE
MOVEMENT

INDOORS LOOKING OUT
by Ariel Ellis

HORSE
by Michaela Smaldone

In this section of the book, you will work with markers. You can make very different types of marks with markers as shown in the student works above.

UNIT 11   balance   Lesson 1

More than One Object

Vocabulary and Creative Exercise

When an arrangement of objects is in balance our eyes move to all the objects and keeps circling through the picture. Here we look at items from a toy box. Because there is as much detail in one object as in another, no one object has our complete attention so we end up looking at all of them in turn.

Explore Your World! A CREATIVE EXERCISE USING REAL-WORLD EXPERIENCE

Each person is unique. Each person's art should reflect that uniqueness. One person might be fascinated with wild animals and draw them. Another studies and draws airplanes. You can explore new ideas for drawings by going to specific areas where different objects of the same kind are already put together. A toy box contains different shaped objects, but with a theme of toy. A kitchen cupboard contains different shaped objects, but all with the theme of container or gadget. Look at bookshelves, tool sheds, coat racks, and other areas for items that are alike.

TRY IT: What new types of objects could you explore? What objects are fun to look at? Arrange three objects in front of you. Overlap them. Draw the group of objects.

OBJECTIVE: to think about personal preferences as a good way to choose subject matter for making art; and to create an image from one's interests.

Looking at Balance in Art   Lesson 2

Art Appreciation

The arrangement of objects, within a picture, need to balance. Just as a real object falls over when it's not balanced, certain objects within the picture space can appear to fall off the page if not connected to other objects. Here the woman's black dress is balanced with the heavy black curtain on the opposite side. The very bright picture is close to center, pulling our eye back to the center and to the women's face.

James Abbott McNeill Whistler (1834 -1903); *Portrait of the Artist's Mother*, 1871
Photo Credit: Dover Publications Inc.

For a moment, don't look at the objects as separate things like a curtain, dress, and so on. Look only at values. You can see balance in the values. In this painting dark values cross from the upper left corner to the lower right. Middle value crosses from the upper right corner to the lower left. White remains near the center.

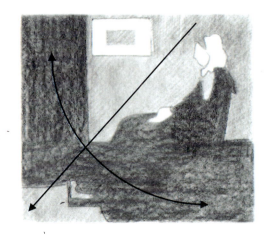

THE ARTIST:
James Abbott McNeill Whistler (1834-1903) American born / British Painter

Whistler was born in America, but had a successful career in Europe as a painter and an etcher. He is known for suing an art critic for a negative review of his artwork. This was unusual because art critics are supposed to inform the public of their honest opinions. He lost the case. He was well known for his biting wit.

THE TIMES:
Before the 20th century, most Americans completed their art training in Europe. There they could see original paintings by master artists that dated back to the early Renaissance period. Some artists, like Whistler, stayed in Europe and made careers there. Famous American artists who made their careers in Europe include John Singleton Copley, Benjamin West, John Singer Sargent, and Mary Cassatt. Despite their stays in Europe, these artists' works appear in books on American art.

MAKE AN OBSERVATION DRAWING! Here we will look at a kitchen tool and use shadows to balance the picture. Using a pencil, start with a neutral ground, as shown on page 39. You will need one strong source of light and a simple background. Arrange the object so that the shadow it creates balances with other dark values. Draw the tool and its shadow. The tool shown below is an egg slicer and its shadow.

1. Create a neutral ground in the middle value range. Draw the outline of the kitchen utensil and its shadow. The shadow is like another object that balances the picture.

2. Lift light areas with an eraser. Here we used a kneaded eraser to get fine lines. You can also shave off a section of a vinyl eraser to make a sharp wedge.

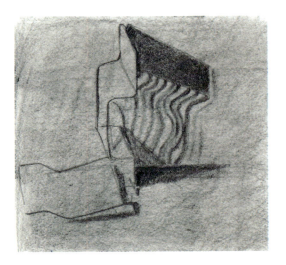
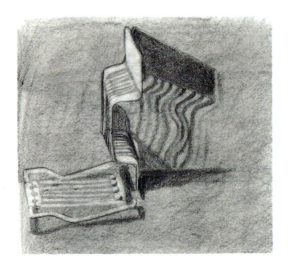

Art History

How to Show Value with a Marker — Lesson 3

Techniques

SHOW VALUE

Leave white space between each line to make value in marker. To make dark values, draw lines close together leaving less white space. To make light values draw lines farther apart. Do NOT press harder on the marker, as you would with a pencil, to get darker values. This will damage the marker tip.

In the marker drawing below, the lines placed closest together create the dark areas inside the doorway. Solid areas of shadow are filled in completely creating the darkest areas. Lines on the wall and on the table are further apart and create lighter areas. Use a ruler to make straighter lines as shown. To use a ruler, place it parallel to the edge of your paper. Hold the ruler with the hand you do not use to draw. Draw a line holding the marker against the edge of the ruler as you pull down. Lift the ruler. Set it where you want and repeat. Notice that the horizontal lines are straight with the top and bottom of the page. The vertical lines are straight with the sides of the page, as shown in the picture below.

Move the ruler away from the line you have just drawn so the ink does not smear.

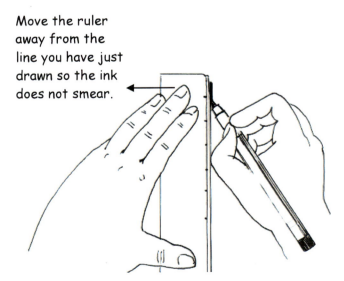

SOMETHING TO TRY: Locate a simple room interior. Draw it using lines further apart for light areas and closer together for dark areas.

Arrange a group of objects by overlapping them. Use balance when drawing the objects on the page by connecting the edges. There are two approaches to take when drawing in marker.

1. Use a pencil to draw light lines to place the objects on the page. Go over the pencil lines with the marker.

2. Draw directly on the paper with marker. Do not be concerned about mistakes, but continue the drawing until you are finished.

Student Gallery

Student work by Aaron Garrison uses pencil and pen in a balanced group of cloth, vegetables, and a container.

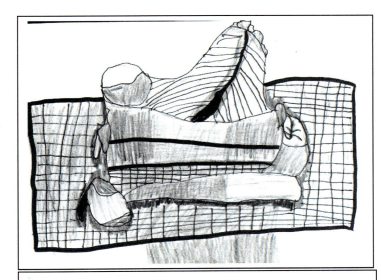

Student work below, by Ariel Ellis, uses the edges of the cloth to wrap around the other objects, assuring balance.

LOOK BACK! Did you balance the group of objects with other objects in the drawing?

Final Project Lesson 4

Application

YOU WILL NEED

- Black ink marker (fine point)
- Black ink marker (broad, flat tip)
- Pencil
- Vinyl eraser
- Paper for Pens
- Drawing board

REFER TO THE FOLLOWING WHEN DRAWING

Use a group of objects, which may be found in the following places:
- Kitchen
- Display shelf
- Play room

UNIT 12   rhythm   Lesson 1

Rhythm is repeating line, shape, value, or any other element within a picture. It helps to draw the eye through the picture space.

Repeating the shape of the balloons

Repeating the lines of the rails

Repeating the dark value of the shirtsleeves.

Vocabulary and Creative Exercise

Explore Your World!   A CREATIVE EXERCISE USING REAL-WORLD EXPERIENCE

Art is a visual record of life. Your parents create a visual record of you when they take photographs of you. They want to remember what you look like at certain ages. George Catlin, the artist we will look at in this unit, painted the native tribes of North America. When Catlin was a boy, he saw Indian cultures vanish from the eastern United States as more people from Europe moved onto the land. He knew this would happen to the western tribes as well. He wanted to record their lives, and did so by making many paintings of tribal activities while living with them. Catlin watched and then worked from the information he saw and remembered. Making artwork from memory teaches us to pay closer attention to things we see.

TRY IT: Your life changes too. Think of something that is in your life now that may not be the same in the next few years. Draw a picture from memory. It may be a scene of a baseball game, family trip, or piano teacher as they instruct a student.

OBJECTIVE: to understand the purpose of art in recording visual information. Practice and improve observation skills through memory drawing.

Looking at Rhythm   Lesson 2

Rhythm catches our attention as we follow repeated lines, shapes, or colors. The distinctive shape of the teepee naturally creates a rhythm. Upon closer observation, the figures, especially their round heads, create another rhythmic pattern that flows in an oval within the bottom half of the painting.

George Catlin (1796-1872) Sioux War Council, c. 1848 Oil on Canvas. 25 ¾ x 32 in.
Photo Credit: Dover Publication Inc., NY.

Rhythmic line in the teepees makes a jagged pattern.

Rhythm created by repeating figures makes a circular shape, drawing our eye throughout the lower half of the painting.

Art History

THE ARTIST:
George Catlin (1796-1872)
American Explorer and Painter

Catlin began his professional career as a portrait painter just forty years after the United States had become a nation. He decided to paint Indian tribes of the West after seeing a group of them traveling to Washington, D.C. When he was a child, his parents welcomed an Indian into their home. Young George was fascinated by the way that the Indian dressed and his mannerisms, but saw that this man seemed very much like them in many ways. From 1830-1836 Catlin traveled thousands of miles, following the trail of Lewis and Clark, and lived among 50 Indian tribes. He painted portraits and scenes of their customs including war, dances, and buffalo hunts on the plains. Later, Catlin traveled even further into unsettled territories to paint the Indians living west of the Rocky Mountains. He also traveled to South America. Although he worked hard to promote the idea of an Indian Gallery so that people could understand their way of life, George Catlin did not see a gallery in his lifetime.

The original paintings for Catlin's Indian Gallery are now housed in the *Smithsonian American Art Museum*. *The National Museum of the American Indian*, established in 1989, and built on the National Mall in Washington D.C. shows Catlin's fine work in one of their displays. His dream of an Indian gallery was finally accomplished.

MAKE AN IMAGINATION DRAWING! Draw a picture of an event where many people are taking the same action. Use rhythm in the picture. It could be a race where people, cars, or bikes line up or a group at an amusement park or theatre.

THE TIMES: Native Americans did not have a tradition of painting or making permanent objects for display. Their art was for sacred purposes, largely unseen, and mobile because most tribes moved frequently. Portrait painting was a European tradition and a few frontiersmen, working independently, were brave enough to meet new tribes, live with them, and paint what they saw. What George Catlin, Seth Eastman, and other explorers brought into their culture was unique. They created the first permanent records of Native American life. You may have heard about a large area of land purchased by the United States of America in 1803. Thomas Jefferson, the third president, did not purchase it from the Native American tribes who lived there, but from the country of France, who had claimed it. It was called the Louisiana Purchase and the area covered most of the Midwest. Jefferson sent Lewis and Clark with fifty other men to explore the area. Their job was to keep journals with pictures of rivers, plants, animals, and the people groups who lived there. It was a time of great discovery and the whole nation was interested in finding out what the land looked like and with whom they shared the land.

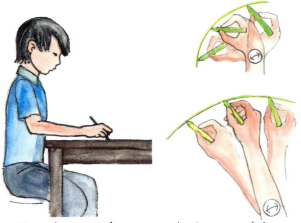

To make smooth curves, pivot your wrist or elbow. Bend at the wrist for small curves. Bend at the elbow for larger curves.

Lesson 3

How to Make Different Marks for Different Effects

When you draw an object, think about the type of marks that would best show the textures of the object. The marks below have different effects. The strong cross hatch lines make a bold effect, while dots make a softer lighter look.

DIFFERENT MARKS FOR DIFFERENT EFFECTS

Use straight lines parallel to each other.

Cross the parallel lines with other parallel lines. This is called cross-hatching.

Use a series of dots or points called pointillism.

Use broken, crooked lines or straight lines made with a ruler.

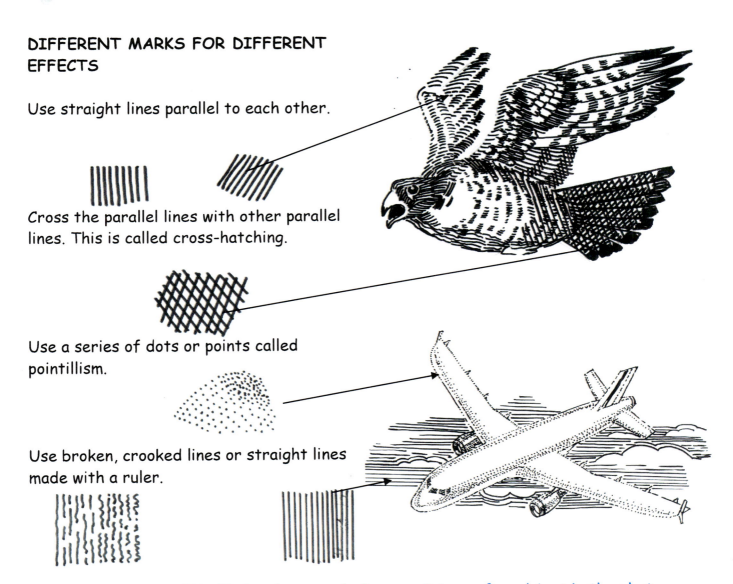

SOMETHING TO TRY: Find a photograph. Draw a picture of an object in the photo. Draw directly on drawing paper with marker or use light pencil marks to place the objects on the page, and then fill in with marker. Use one or more methods of making value as shown above.

Walk in your neighborhood or other area. Notice patterns or repeated elements that create rhythms. Look in the distance as well as up close. A fence, brick wall, flock of geese, or yard full of dandelions can become the source of rhythm for a drawing. Create a drawing with rhythm.

Final Project Lesson 4

Student Gallery

The student work above, by Aaron Johns, uses marks to show rhythm. Lines, dots, and shapes in the clouds are used to make rhythm. Haylee Raymond repeats the tree shape in the work below to create rhythm.

YOU WILL NEED

- Black ink marker (point)
- Black ink marker (broad, flat tip)
- Pencil
- Vinyl eraser
- Paper for Pens
- Drawing board

REFER TO THE FOLLOWING WHEN DRAWING

Choose a scene that you see while walking through your neighborhood. Look for one or more repeated elements.

LOOK BACK! What parts of your picture show rhythm? What are the elements that are repeated?

The Elements Combined: Solid and Textured Areas

This additional lesson shows how you might use solid and textured areas to best represent your subject. These techniques can be used with any subject. Choose your own subject and follow the steps on this page.

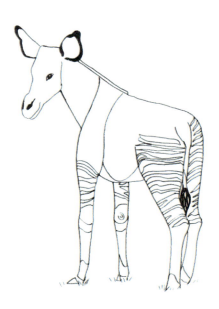

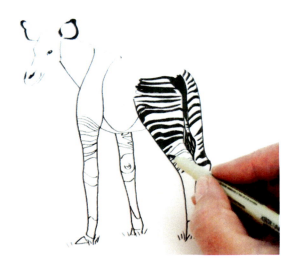

The edges of the object are drawn with a pencil, then, outlined with a fine point marker. This marker is used to fill in small areas like the stripes.

A wide flat tip is used to fill in solid areas. When filling in a solid area, overlap the marks slightly so that the white of the paper does not show through. The finished work shows texture with lines and dots and solid areas of black.

UNIT 13 overlap Lesson 1

Vocabulary and Creative Exercise

When one object moves in front of another, blocking part of the other object from view, it **overlaps.** One way to achieve balance is to overlap objects and connect the edges as shown on the right.

Explore Your World! A CREATIVE EXERCISE USING REAL-WORLD EXPERIENCE

Sometimes an artist uses a subject in their work simply because they like it. Many people prefer hanging pictures of food or fruit in their kitchen, or flowers and landscapes in their living room. Some like to hang pictures of people they know on their walls. The next time someone asks your reason for drawing a particular thing, simply say it is because you like it. Ralph Waldo Emerson stated, "Every genuine work of art has as much reason for being as the earth and the sun." We all understand the earth and sun as things we could not live without.

TRY IT: Choose several objects from your room that you are fond of. Arrange them and draw a picture of them.

OBJECTIVE: to use personal preference as a guide for choosing subject matter.

Looking at Overlap   Lesson 2

When one object is in front of another and hides part of the object that is behind, we say that the two objects overlap. Overlap takes place from one point of view. This scene of a parade shows many overlapping flags. Overlapping is like a chain that links the shapes together.

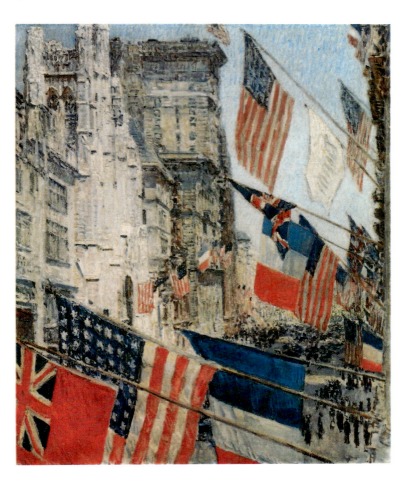

Childe Hassam (1859-1935), *Allies Day, May, 1917.*
Photo Credit: Dover Publications Inc.

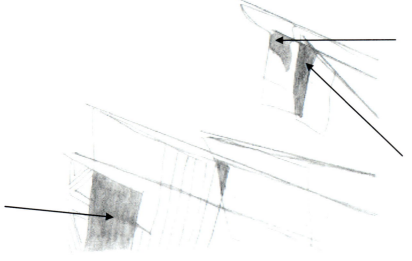

The British flag overlaps the American flag. The area where they overlap is shaded in here.

Three flags overlap. The British flag overlaps a portion of the blue and white area of the French flag. The French flag overlaps the upper portion of the American flag.

71

Art Appreciation

THE ARTIST:
Frederick Childe Hassam (1859-1935) American Impressionist Painter

Hassam studied in Europe for a time, but returned to New York to paint scenes of the life he saw on the streets and in homes. Hassam is famous for his series of 22 flag paintings. He began these before World War I started. The event that inspired him to paint flags was a "Preparedness Parade" held on Fifth Avenue in New York. Hassam's flag paintings all take place on Fifth Avenue or Fifty-Seventh Street, near his gallery. In the painting, *Allies Day, May 1917* we see the American flag and flags of those nations America would fight alongside, Great Britain and France.

THE TIMES:
American Impressionism is the term given to those who lived in America and copied the techniques of Impressionism. These techniques included loosely applied brush strokes and intense color. Americans became aware of this style in the 1880's when Impressionist art from Europe was displayed in Boston and New York. The movement had started twenty years earlier. Impressionism appealed to the tastes of the American public long before it was widely enjoyed in Europe, where it first started. Impressionism inspired artist's colonies to sprout up in small American towns. There artists could paint the American scenery and live relatively cheaply. Groups of artists who thought alike could get together to talk about what they were painting and express new ideas. Today one still finds art colonies and centers throughout the United States where artists gather for fellowship and inspiration.

MAKE AN OBSERVATION DRAWING!
When the world seems cluttered with too much information, you can block out the uninteresting information and find a view that is balanced. Look through a viewfinder to border what you see and locate a good composition. Measure, draw and cut a two-inch border within a sheet of black construction paper. Hold the viewfinder up and look for good compositions within your frame. Once a good arrangement is found, begin to draw. Hold up the viewfinder and refer to the view through the viewfinder as needed, while drawing.

Cut one piece or glue two pieces together.

How to Arrange a Still Life   Lesson 3

Techniques

> What is a still life? A still life is a group of objects that are inanimate or not moving. These objects stay still while you draw them and can include anything. They are usually objects that are smaller than a car.

To arrange good lighting for a still life, a table is set in front of a window. The artist sits with his or her side to the window. The drawing board and objects are in front. The form will be clear if the objects are arranged so that both a light side and a shaded side are seen.

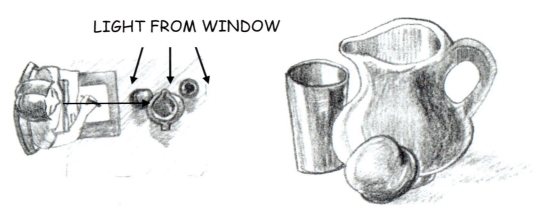

LIGHT FROM WINDOW

SOMETHING TO TRY: Arrange a still life using two or three simply shaped objects. Overlap them, keeping the smallest objects in front or in view. Overlapping makes the subject more interesting to look at.

NO OVERLAP   OBJECTS OVERLAP

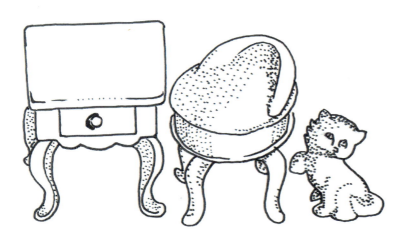

73

Fruits and vegetables are fun to draw because of their shapes. Arrange a pile of them to draw. Look carefully at the overlapping shapes and concentrate as you draw them.

Student Gallery

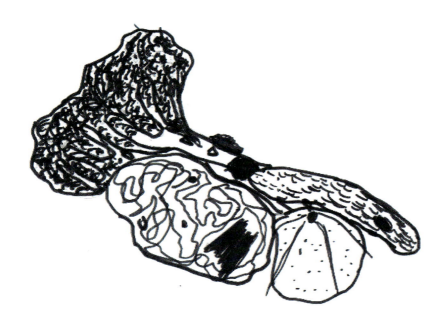

Student work by Bethany Krebs shows overlap.

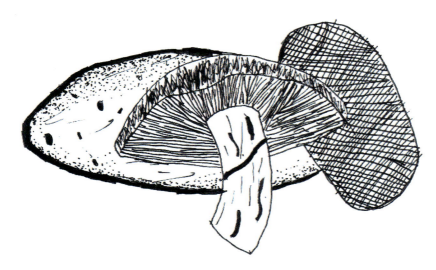

Student work by Laura Smith shows overlap.

LOOK BACK! Did you overlap objects in the drawing?

Final Project Lesson 4

Application

YOU WILL NEED

- Black ink marker (fine point)
- Black ink marker (broad, flat tip)
- Pencil
- Vinyl eraser
- Paper for Pens
- Drawing board

REFER TO THE FOLLOWING WHEN DRAWING

Arrange vegetables or fruits, stacked in a small pile.

UNIT 14   depth   Lesson 1

Vocabulary and Creative Exercise

Depth is a measurement from front to back. The foreground is the front of the picture. The middle ground is in the center of the picture. The background is the back of the picture. The tadpoles are in the foreground. The large frog is in the middle ground. What do you see in the background?

Photo Credit: Dover Publications Inc.

Explore Your World! A CREATIVE EXERCISE USING REAL-WORLD EXPERIENCE

Sometimes a simple change in the materials you use can open up a new awareness of what you see. This can be true when you reverse the drawing process by drawing white on black paper. The things you normally "fill in" when using a regular pencil will not be filled in with a white pencil. Instead, you may leave the black paper showing in those areas. A daylight sky, which you may be used to leaving white, now has to be drawn in with the white pencil. This reverse thinking is both challenging and fun.

TRY IT: Work on black paper with a white pencil. Observe a single subject and draw it up close and at a distance. The object can vary in its shape. Do more than just a line drawing. Fill in areas with texture and shading, just as you would with a regular drawing.

OBJECTIVE: to use the idea of depth in whatever way the student perceives it and to create a work on black paper, causing the student to rethink how to show values.

Looking at Depth   Lesson 2

William Glackens (1870-1938), *Mahone Bay; 1911*. Photo Credit: Dover Publications Inc.

In this painting by William Glackens, we see how objects appear to get smaller the further in the distance they are. The figures in the foreground (bottom of the painting) are larger than the figures in the background (end of the pier). The ships follow the same formula: appearing smaller as they recede in the distance.

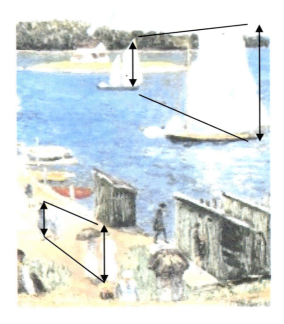

Art History

THE ARTIST:
William James Glackens (1870-1938)
American Realist Painter

Glackens co-founded the Ashcan school movement in New York City. He wanted to paint the reality of living in a large city. People were not used to seeing low-income families as being worthy subject matter for painting, so his works were not liked by some. The city's neighborhoods, back streets, and back yards were not considered beautiful places. However, Glackens wanted to show reality, and the good side of people and places that were not so beautiful. Glackens studied in Europe for a time. Later he went to Cuba as a combat artist for a magazine to make illustrations of the stories of Teddy Roosevelt's Rough Riders (McLanathan396).

THE TIMES: Glackens and his friends were young newspaper artists who worked with a jolly art teacher, Robert Henri. As newspaper artists, they had to draw realistic portrayals of what went on in real life in order to illustrate each news story (McLanathan 395). They brought that interest to their painting. When their paintings were rejected by the annual National Academy exhibition, they and Henri held an independent show called, "Eight American Painters". They were later referred to as The Eight and as the Ashcan school. The Ashcan school is a negative term for painting the sometimes gritty reality of city life. By today's standards, their works were positive. They showed people of all kinds, focusing on those at work and at play. William Glackens' painting, *Mahone Bay*, points to the lighter, brighter side of life.

MAKE A MEMORY DRAWING: What happens in your back yard? Think about what your back yard looks like. Notice depth. Draw things in the foreground, middle ground, and background.

This picture shows how pine trees of the same size appear smaller the further away they sit from the viewer. This is one way to show depth.

How to use Hatch Lines

Lesson 3

Techniques

Use a pointed marker to make single hatch lines. Cross over the lines to make double hatch lines. Add darker values by adding more lines until the area is near black.

Single-hatching

Double-hatching

Triple-hatching

Near-black

Black

Use the wide tip marker to make solid black areas.

Objects that are near should be drawn in detail. Tree leaves in the picture below are large, showing more detail. Trees in the background show less detail. The figure in the foreground shows more detail, while the figure in the background is less detailed.

Grass is drawn with single lines in the background. More lines are added near the foreground, making it darker.

The dots in the path become closer together and darker in the foreground.

SOMETHING TO TRY: Draw a scene showing distance. Build up dark areas starting with single lines, then double-hatching, triple-hatching, near-black, and black as shown.

78

Go outdoors to look for scenes with depth. If you live in the city, it is sometimes difficult to see far into the distance. Locate an area where you can see a background, not necessarily the horizon. A view down a street or alley will allow you to see into the distance and will give you an opportunity to draw with perspective. Notice the diminishing size of objects to create depth in the drawing.

Final Project Lesson 4

Application

What is a landscape? A landscape is any view of the land. It can include anything one might see when looking outdoors. Landscapes have trees, mountains, water, buildings, animals, or even people.

Student Gallery

In this student work by Laura Smith, the landscape clearly shows foreground, middle ground, and background. The fence marks the foreground. The row of houses marks the middle ground. The mountains mark the background.

LOOK BACK! Does the drawing show foreground, middle ground, and background? What objects are found in each area?

YOU WILL NEED

- Black ink marker (fine point)
- Black ink marker (broad, flat tip)
- Pencil
- Vinyl eraser
- Paper
- Drawing board

REFER TO THE FOLLOWING WHEN DRAWING

Look outdoors. Find a view from real life in which you can see foreground, middle ground, and background. Look for perspective lines also.

UNIT 15 proportion, the face Lesson 1

Vocabulary and Creative Exercise

Proportion is the correct relationship of the parts of an object. For correct proportion on a face, the eyes sit half way between the top of the head and the chin. This is the same when the head is turned to the side or seen from a front view.

Explore Your World!   A CREATIVE EXERCISE USING REAL-WORLD EXPERIENCE

Artists often make portraits in order to say something about the person. This makes the artistic portrait different from portraits taken in most photographers' studios. There the backdrop is chosen out of a few available and has nothing to do with the person. The artist, however, often includes objects beside and behind the person. These objects tell us something about the person. Look at the portrait of the couple in *American Gothic* on the next page. What can you tell about these people? What clues has the artist used to tell you those things? If these people dressed up and went to a photography studio, would you know as much about them?

TRY IT: Draw a portrait of yourself at work, play, or surrounded by something important to you. Think about what you want to say about yourself. Give clues by placing objects in the portrait that will tell the viewer about you. Work from your imagination.

OBJECTIVE: to use imagination to compose a picture about the artist. The assignment develops imaginary preplanning skills as the student decides which objects to include in the picture that will best say something about who he or she is.

Looking at the Face   Lesson 2

A painted portrait usually captures more about a person than just what they look like. The portrait below is loved by many because it gives us a look into rural America in the mid 1900's. In *American Gothic*, Grant Wood captured more than the physical features of this farmer and his daughter. Their eyes show a serious, hard working attitude. The house and clothing show order and neatness. The pitchfork placed in the farmer's hands shows that the Midwest farmer is a hard worker.

Art Appreciation

Grant Wood (1892-1942), *American Gothic*, 1930.
Photo Credit: Dover Publications Inc.

The background tells us that they are neat, tidy people.

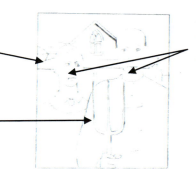

The clothing is not expensive, but is neatly pressed. The farmer wears a jacket over his overalls, telling us that he is a hard worker. An object placed in the hand, like this pitchfork, tells us his occupation.

The expressions give the painting a serious tone. The straight line of the lips offers no suggestion of a smile. This tells us that these two take life seriously.

Art History

THE ARTIST: Grant Wood (1892-1942)
American Regionalist Artist

Wood was known for his paintings of farming communities in the Midwest. He was a leading figure in a movement known as Regionalism. This movement dominated American art in the 1930's. Wood rejected the new modern approach and came to believe that artists should remain in their hometowns rather than move to New York. He thought artists should paint their experiences based on their local heritage. While working as a teacher he painted landscapes of the Midwest, portraits of local characters, and famous scenes from American history.

THE ART:
American Gothic is perhaps the most famous portrait painting in the history of American art. It was shown in 1930 for the first time at the Art Institute of Chicago. It created quite an uproar. Some felt Wood was mocking the rural Midwestern lifestyle. Others felt he was glorifying the virtues of hard work and tidiness that typified the American farmer. Wood claimed that it was not meant to be seen as derogatory. He'd seen the old house and wanted to paint the typical American family. This is really a made-up family. He asked his dentist and daughter to pose for the painting. He intentionally dressed him as a farmer using the overalls that were the common work clothes of that time. The daughter is dressed in a modest dress with rickrack neatly lining the edges of her apron.

THE TIMES: Many movements in art began in Europe. Americans picked up the same ideas by traveling to Europe and by viewing art shows from Europe that traveled to America. Regionalism was different. It was a purely American movement. The Regionalists were very aware of the Abstract movement that began in Europe and was now being embraced by Americans. Grant Wood had studied in the best American schools and in Europe. For a time he was involved with the new and sometimes absurd ideas being explored there. One group sat around and waited for the next big, new idea to come. Not many ideas happen when one does nothing but wait. This experience changed Wood's ideas about what art should be. He said that his good ideas all came while milking a cow (while he was working), not by sitting around. Once he returned to America, he began making art that was purely about the work ethic and beliefs of Americans. Regionalism, a group connected only by their conservative views, was a movement that aggressively opposed European abstract art. They wanted to show rural American subjects in a realistic style that anyone could understand. People certainly did feel something toward this type of art. Today representational works of art by Norman Rockwell, Grant Wood, and Thomas Hart Benton are some of the best-loved art works in the nation.

MAKE AN IMAGINATION DRAWING: Draw a portrait of yourself and a family member. Place things in the background that show the viewer something about you and the family member like what you do or where you live.

How to Draw the Face

Lesson 3
Techniques

When drawing a difficult subject in marker, you can draw in pencil first. Draw light lines that can be erased easily. Make changes as needed. When you have everything in place, draw over the pencil lines with your marker. Once you finish, erase any pencil lines that still show.

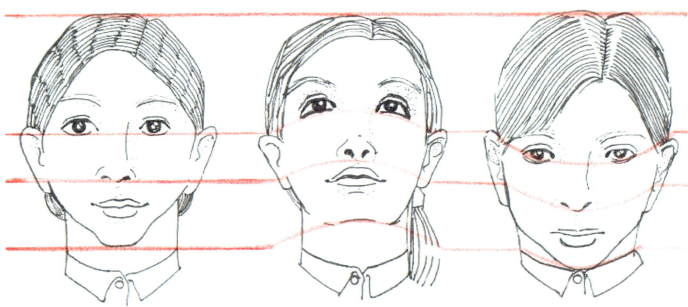

When viewed straight on (left) the eyes sit on the center line between the top of the head and the chin. The base of the nose is centered between the eyes and chin. The line of the mouth sits between the nose and chin. When viewed from a low angle, (center) the eyes, nose, and mouth curve upward. Less of the hair is seen. The chin is lifted, showing more of the neck. When viewed from a high angle, (right) the eyes, nose, and mouth curve downward. More of the hair is seen. The chin meets the collar.

SOMETHING TO TRY: Look at your face in a mirror. Turn your head slightly to the left, right, up, or down and draw what you see. The best way to draw faces is to observe them directly.

Draw a person you do not know personally, but that you admire and know something about. It may be a sports star, a famous person from any occupation, or a historical figure. Find a photo of the person from books, newspapers, or an encyclopedia. You may want to include surroundings that tell the viewer about that person.

Final Project Lesson 4

Application

Student Gallery

Student work by Ariel Ellis shows a portrait of George Washington, American hero. Here she uses the markers in different ways such as lines, dots, thick line.

YOU WILL NEED

- Black ink marker (fine point)
- Black ink marker (broad, flat tip)
- Pencil
- Vinyl eraser
- Paper for Pens
- Drawing board

REFER TO THE FOLLOWING WHEN DRAWING

Use a photo of a famous person from a newspaper, magazine, book, or encyclopedia.

LOOK BACK! What is the picture telling about the person? How does the portrait show this information?

The Elements Combined: Lines, Forms, and Values

This additional lesson shows how you might put marks into a picture of a person using fine and broad tip markers. These techniques can be used with any subject. Choose your own subject and follow the steps on this page.

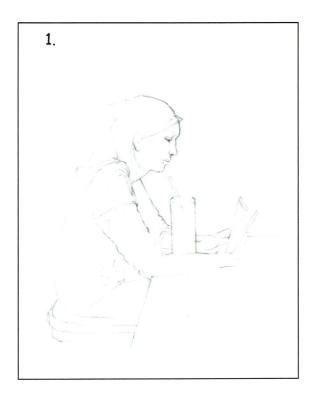

1. Since the marker cannot be erased, the drawing is started in pencil. All corrections in the drawing are made at this step. 2. Fine lines are then laid in with a #1 pointed marker, in the direction that best shows the form. Lines tend to wrap around round forms like the head, arm and torso. Hatching and cross-hatching are used to make light and dark values. 3. Once all the values are in place, a #2 wide tip marker is used to make the broad stripes on the hoodie. Each stripe is made with one stroke. The wide marker is used to fill the solid black space for the pants, creating the darkest area of the picture.

UNIT 16 movement Lesson 1

Vocabulary and Creative Exercise

Movement is the illusion of motion we give to a subject. We know that a picture on a piece of paper does not move, but when drawn with certain things in mind, the illusion of motion can be created. The tail in the air and the legs stretched out from under the Greater Kudu show that it is moving forward at a fast pace.

Photo Credit: Dover Publications Inc.

Explore Your World! A CREATIVE EXERCISE USING REAL-WORLD EXPERIENCE

Artists use their imaginations when making art. When images are thought up in the mind, they quickly disappear, just as a dream disappears moments after waking. By drawing the things imagined, a record is kept on paper that will not disappear.

Most of us know what Peter Rabbit looks like in his little blue jacket. This is because the person who imagined him first in a coat and shoes also drew a picture of him to be shared with others. She observed real rabbits and then boldly stood her creation on his hind legs! This character can be found in the book, *The Tale of Peter Rabbit,* by Beatrix Potter. You may enjoy the 2007 movie of the life story of Miss Potter, called *MISS POTTER.*

TRY IT: Observe a real animal. If none is available, use a picture of one. Take a few moments to form a character in your mind, based on your observations. Draw the character onto paper. You will discover how observation and imagination work together.

OBJECTIVE: to use observation and imagination for developing an original character.

Looking at Movement   Lesson 2

Art often carries a message. At fourteen, Brook Watson had a frightful experience with sharks. He later had this painting made to tell other young men not to make his mistake. He was a sailor on a ship, docked in the Havana Harbor. On a very hot day, he took off the heavy wool sailor's uniform, as was customary in that day, and went for a swim. While he was in the water he fell prey to sharks. Sailors from his ship came to his rescue. He escaped, losing only his foot. He never forgot the experience. Later in his life, he hired John Copley, a well-known portrait artist, to paint a picture of the event. The painting Copley created shows everyone in motion as they try to rescue Brook Watson. Do you see how their arms stretch out?

John Singleton Copley (1738-1815). *Watson and the Shark*. 1778.
Photo Credit: Dover Publications Inc.

A rope has been thrown to Watson. Is it clear what his outcome will be? The artist has stopped the action at the highest point of tension. We don't know, by looking at the painting, if the shark will swallow Watson in the next moment or if Watson will grab hold of the rope that has fallen across his arm, and be pulled to freedom.

THE ARTIST:
John Singleton Copley
American Portrait Artist (1738-1815)

Copley was born near Boston. He was considered the greatest portrait painter in colonial America. His stepfather was an engraver and painter who inspired him to become an artist at an early age. He began his career painting historical works. It was his lifelong ambition to paint the heroes of America. After his popularity grew he moved to Europe, painting elegant portraits and current events.

THE ART OF A NATION:

Perhaps the study of movement is the perfect final chapter to our look at American art. Americans have always been a people on the go, exploring new ideas and new ways of doing things. America was founded by people who had moved from other countries in order to practice religious freedom. They took risks as they came by ship to a new land and attempted to make homes on the North American continent. This view of religious freedom was best captured in the art of Edward Hicks. His *Peaceable Kingdom* series shows an ideal world with wild animals, tame animals, and children lounging peacefully together. The background shows how the Quakers practiced peace by purchasing land from Native Americans, rather than taking it. Paul Revere explored new ideas of freedom of speech in the artwork, *Boston Massacre*. It makes sense that Americans, who were not afraid to explore the ideas of a totally new kind of government, were also not afraid to explore in numerous other ways. We looked at explorer artist, George Catlin. He lived with the native peoples of this continent and used canvas and paint to capture their faces and their practices for the first time. We looked at frontier artist Fredrick Remington. He traveled west to paint the Cowboys. Nature artist, James Audubon, explored many parts of North America to paint the wildlife. Folk artists like Milton William Hopkins traveled throughout the early settlements as Americans moved west and displayed a do-it-yourself attitude as they created whatever type of art was needed without formal training. America is nation of diverse people. Many traveled here to escape persecution, famine, or other difficulties of life with the hope of building the new life they envisioned. Others worked hard to claim that freedom on American soil long after their ancestors had been transported to America as slaves. The travelers come from many lands and have come continually for 400 years. The art they make expresses their ideas of freedom and exploration. In the next book, we will look at more adventurous American artists, who moved art into new directions and unexplored territories.

MAKE AN OBSERVATION DRAWING:
Visit a zoo or other public place to draw people and animals in motion. Draw with markers.

How to Use a Grid
Lesson 3

A grid is one way to see accurate proportions when drawing from a photograph. Look at each section, comparing your drawing to the original. You can increase or decrease the size of the object by increasing or decreasing the size of the squares.

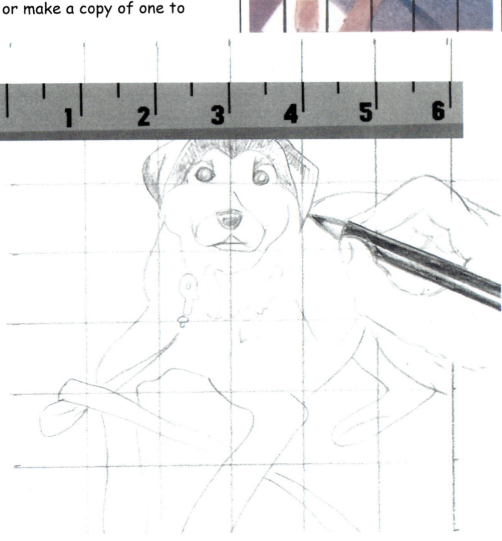

Use a large photograph or make a copy of one to draw the grid lines onto. To draw grid lines, mark the picture into ½-inch sections. Use a ruler. Mark a dot at each ½ inch on the top and the bottom of the photograph. Then draw parallel lines connecting the marks. Do the same for the sides. To make a drawing twice as large as an original picture, make the same amount of lines, this time measuring them one inch apart. To draw, look at what is happening in each square. Draw it. Erase the grid lines once the drawing is completed.

SOMETHING TO TRY: Find a picture that you can draw lines on. Use the method shown on this page to draw a picture similar to the photograph. Finish the drawing in marker.

Compare the still bird to the bird in motion. What do you notice about the bird that shows movement? Do you see how the limbs are spread out? The faster one moves the further the limbs spread from the body.

Photo Credit: Dover Publications Inc.

Draw an animal that is in motion from a photograph. It is important to take time to choose a photograph that clearly shows details of the animal. If you enjoyed using a grid, use one in this assignment as well.

Student Gallery

Student works above by Laura Smith. The bird shows movement.

Final Project Lesson 4

Application

YOU WILL NEED

- Black ink marker (fine point)
- Black ink marker (broad, flat tip)
- Pencil
- Vinyl eraser
- Paper for Pens
- Drawing board

REFER TO THE FOLLOWING WHEN DRAWING

Use a photograph of an animal in motion, observing carefully as you draw. Look for a calendar or magazine picture.

LOOK BACK! Did you observe the proportion of the animal? Did you draw more than an outline, showing the form of the animal?

90

Evaluation Sheet
FOR OBTAINING A NUMBER AND LETTER GRADE

Teachers may calculate a number and letter grade for each project within each unit. Follow the instructions below as you look at the final work. DO NOT take off points for concepts not yet taught. Follow the objectives carefully when grading.

Because of art's subjective qualities it is best to mark higher rather than lower when deciding between two levels of achievement. If the student enjoys doing the lessons and has made the effort to create a work of art in a thoughtful way, then that student should be given a good grade. Allow the student to grow into mature artistic expression. Do not demand results that can only be obtained by repeated experience that the student has not yet had. It is very likely that an individual who enjoys making art will get A's. This does not mean that the student has arrived at a full knowledge and use of artistic concepts. It does mean the student is doing well in the pursuit of that goal.

LEVELS OF ACHIEVEMENT Choose the number of points that most accurately describes the work from each of the three categories below. Add the numbers from categories 1, 2, 3, and 4. This is the student's total score for the unit. This number can be translated into a letter grade: 90-100 (A) 80-89 (B) 70-79 (C) Incomplete work (D-F).

Note: If you do not see how the student accomplished the objectives asked for, **do ask them about it**. Sometimes they understand very well and will be able to tell you how they accomplished the task in the drawing. This is valid. Remember that getting a visual idea across clearly is a process that takes time. Allow the student to grow into it.

1. Explore Your World	2. Make a Drawing	3. Something to Try	4. Final Project
25 POINTS/ COMPLETED ASSIGNMENT AND OBTAINED ALL OBJECTIVES IN GOLD BOX AT THE BOTTOM OF THE PAGE	25 POINTS/ COMPLETED ASSIGNMENT IN BLUE SHOWS GOOD UNDERSTANDING OF CONCEPT SHOWN IN ART WORK	25 POINTS/ COMPLETED ASSIGNMENT IN BLUE SHOWS GOOD UNDERSTANDING AND USE OF MATERIALS OR TECHNIQUES	25 POINTS/ COMPLETED PROJECT SHOWS GOOD UNDERSTANDING OF THE UNIT (SEE TITLE) AND USE OF THOSE ITEMS ASKED FOR IN THE BLUE BOX AT THE BOTTOM OF THE PAGE
20 POINTS/ COMPLETED ASSIGNMENT AND OBTAINED SOME OF THE OBJECTIVES IN GOLD BOX AT THE BOTTOM OF THE PAGE	20 POINTS/ COMPLETED ASSIGNMENT IN BLUE SHOWS AN ATTEMPT TO USE CONCEPT SHOWN IN ART WORK	20 POINTS/ COMPLETED ASSIGNMENT IN BLUE SHOWS AN ATTEMPT TO USE MATERIALS OR TECHNIQUES	20POINTS/ COMPLETED PROJECT SHOWS UNDERSTANDING OF UNIT BUT DID NOT ACCOMPLISH SOME ITEMS ASKED FOR IN THE BLUE BOX AT THE BOTTOM OF THE PAGE
15 POINTS/ COMPLETED ASSIGNMENT BUT DID NOT OBTAIN OBJECTIVES IN THE GOLD BOX AT THE BOTTOM OF THE PAGE	15 POINTS/ COMPLETED ASSIGNMENT IN BLUE DID NOT USE CONCEPT SHOWN IN ART WORK	15 POINTS/ COMPLETED ASSIGNMENT IN BLUE DID NOT USE MATERIALS CORRECTLY OR TRY THE TECHNIQUE SHOWN	15 POINTS/ COMPLETED PROJECT DID NOT SHOW UNDERSTANDING OF UNIT OR ITEMS IN BLUE BOX AT THE BOTTOM OF THE PAGE

BIBLIOGRAPHY

Batterberry, Ariane Ruskin and Michael. *The Pantheon Story of American Art for Young People.* Pantheon Books, USA, 1976.

D'Ambrosio, Paul S. The Erie Canal and New York State Folk Art. <u>Magazine Antiques</u>, (April 1999). Retrieved November 26, 2007, from BNet Research Center on-line database (http://findarticles.com/p/articles/mi_m1026/is_4_155/ai_54370845).

Hirsch, E. D. Jr. *What Your 5th Grader Needs to Know, Fundamentals of a Good Fifth Grade Education,* The Core Knowledge Series, Doubleday, New York, NY 1993.

McLanathan, Richard. *The American Tradition in the Arts.* Harcourt Brace Jovanovich Inc, New York 1968.

Powell, Jim. Ideas on Liberty. *William Penn, America's First Great Champion for Liberty and Peace.* Reprinted on www.quaker.org by permission. Retrieved October24, 2007.

Von Oech, Roger. *A Whack on the Side of the Head, How You Can Be More Creative.* MJF Books, New York, NY 1998.

Wright, Tricia. *Smithsonian Q&A, The Ultimate Question and Answer Book, American Art and Artists.* Produced for HarperCollins by: Hydra Publishing, NY 2007.